CW00664606

Fashion and Family History

To Pippa Christmas 2020
Lots of love Dad xxxxx

Fashion and Family History

Interpreting How Your Ancestors Dressed

Jayne Shrimpton

Pen & Sword
FAMILY HISTORY

First published in Great Britain in 2020 by
Pen & Sword Family History
An imprint of
Pen & Sword Books Ltd
Yorkshire – Philadelphia

Copyright © Jayne Shrimpton 2020

ISBN 978 1 52676 026 5

The right of Jayne Shrimpton to be identified as Author of this
work has been asserted by her in accordance with the Copyright,
Designs and Patents Act 1988.

A CIP catalogue record for this book is
available from the British Library.

All rights reserved. No part of this book may be reproduced
or transmitted in any form or by any means, electronic or
mechanical including photocopying, recording or by any
information storage and retrieval system, without permission
from the Publisher in writing.

Typeset by Mac Style
Printed and bound in the UK by TJ Books Ltd,
Padstow, Cornwall.

Pen & Sword Books Limited incorporates the imprints of Atlas,
Archaeology, Aviation, Discovery, Family History, Fiction,
History, Maritime, Military, Military Classics, Politics, Select,
Transport, True Crime, Air World, Frontline Publishing, Leo
Cooper, Remember When, Seaforth Publishing, The Praetorian
Press, Wharncliffe Local History, Wharncliffe Transport,
Wharncliffe True Crime and White Owl.

For a complete list of Pen & Sword titles please contact

PEN & SWORD BOOKS LIMITED
47 Church Street, Barnsley, South Yorkshire, S70 2AS, England
E-mail: enquiries@pen-and-sword.co.uk
Website: www.pen-and-sword.co.uk

Or

PEN AND SWORD BOOKS
1950 Lawrence Rd, Havertown, PA 19083, USA
E-mail: Uspen-and-sword@casematepublishers.com
Website: www.penandswordbooks.com

Contents

Acknowledgements

This book is for everyone and since it represents over thirty years' professional experience, many people have contributed content in different ways. I am especially grateful to friends and contacts who have permitted me to include images and heirlooms from their own collections. I should also like to thank Amy Jordan at Pen & Sword Books, for her endless patience and professional support.

Picture Credits

Ron Cosens/www.cartedevisite.co.uk: 20, 52–53, 78, 80; colour plates 6, 9–10

James Morley: 3–4, 14, 43, 70, 73; colour plates 5(a) & (b)

Simon Martin: 13, 22, 24, 31, 69, 72, 91; colour plate 4

Katharine Williams: 9–10, 28, 33, 38, 58, 64, 67

Remaining images are from the author's collection or are in the public domain

Introduction

'Fashion' might seem a frivolous subject, yet studying dress is relevant to family history in many ways. Generally speaking, knowing what people looked like in a given period – what clothes and hairstyles they wore, for example, in the Regency era or during the 1890s – helps with envisaging life in those times. As an art, dress and photographic historian, my belief in the value of accurate pictorial material underpins the strong visual emphasis to this book. Part of its aim is to provide informative and inspirational contextual illustrations in the form of historical prints, paintings, photographs and advertisements; often absent from documentary-based genealogical research, these images bring us literally face to face with our past.

This study focuses on dress in Britain from 1800 until 1950 – a critical period spanning the so-called 'Industrial Revolution' that transformed the nation from a traditional agrarian society to an urban, industrial society and the aftermath of the Second World War. This timeframe encompasses our families' relatively recent histories, beginning with ancestors born around six to eight generations ago and ending around the time that we, or our parents, were born. Rich source material reveals how fashion and dress accelerated throughout those 150 years, responding to a changing economy and society, reflecting evolving tastes and needs, new intellectual ideas and advancing technology, and the rise of modern popular culture.

Many people living during the nineteenth and early/mid-twentieth centuries would have been far removed from the luxury high-end modes emanating from Paris (the source of western style); yet looking back, we observe how major sartorial trends representing progress – for example, the adoption of female trousers – do gradually gain in popularity and become widely established. It is also evident that the fashions prevailing at any given time influence the form and development of all types of clothes, even uniforms and the purposefully 'anti-fashion' garments that minority groups adopt. Fashion is an inescapable aspect of human existence.

Exploring our ancestors' relationship with dress helps us to understand their daily lives more clearly than many other avenues of historical investigation. Dressing in the morning, attending to personal grooming, selecting work or leisure wear, shopping for clothes, painstakingly sewing or knitting garments, dressing up for special occasions, packing for holidays, being photographed in favourite outfits – or budgeting to clothe a large family; these intimate, intensely human routines and rituals, joys and challenges represent time-honoured experiences, connecting the generations in familiar ways.

Everyone has to wear clothes for basic modesty, protection, warmth and comfort, but throughout history dress has also served to demonstrate a person's age, gender, social status, occupation and place in the world, signifying who they are – or perhaps how they want to appear. Work wear has featured prominently for most people, with standardised outfits or official uniforms characterising some occupations. Throughout time it has also been considered important to present a respectable public appearance, although some have struggled, through poverty, to maintain a decent wardrobe.

Over time, particular forms of dress have symbolised important individual, family and community rituals, reflecting recognised rites of passage and certain occasions: some special clothing customs have survived to the present day, such as bridalwear, while others, like prescribed mourning attire, represent obsolete traditions. Conversely, other types of outfit evolved almost beyond recognition throughout our period, particularly holiday and sports wear – relaxed, easy-fitting clothes offering respite from the strictures of formal fashion.

Examining dress, its acquisition and preservation reveals much about our predecessors' economic circumstances, their shopping habits and skills with needle or machine. Compared with today's easy access to fashion and ready-made disposable goods, clothing played a heightened role in the past, when every dress item was a carefully considered purchase, its price, quality, durability and overall value weighed up in relation to its intended purpose. Lengths of cloth for making up into garments, complete clothes, their trimmings and accessories all had an intrinsic worth: they were precious commodities, valuable personal property. The clothing of the poor usually comprised the majority of their material possessions; a form of portable wealth, jewellery, garments and accessories were readily exchanged for money. In most families, clothes and footwear were expected to last and were looked after until they could no longer be worn.

Earlier generations understood different textiles and their properties, what fabric best suited different garments and how clothes and accessories must be washed, ironed, stored and renovated. Traditionally most females learned to sew, and until the second-half of the twentieth century the women of the house often stitched or knitted some of the family's clothes. Women (and some men) diligently altered, refurbished and mended dress items and had boots and shoes regularly repaired. The further back in time we travel, the more complex and time-consuming was assembling and maintaining a wardrobe.

Textile and clothing production used to occupy a significant place in the British economy and many of our forebears earned a living working in fashion-related industries, from lace-makers, seamstresses and washerwomen to cotton mill hands, hatters and boot-makers. Investigating ancestors' occupational backgrounds often reveals such trades, their geographical location typically linked to particular manufactures. Advancing mechanisation and mass-production during our period hastened and facilitated many industrial processes, making fashionable dress affordable for more ordinary people and changing the nature of many jobs. However, the historic importance of traditional roles lives on in many surnames: Mercer, Draper, Fuller, Glover and Tanner to mention but a few.

We may well wonder about the clothes that our predecessors wore, what fashion-related tasks they undertook and how they felt about their appearance. My late father recalled that he was the first youth in his North London street to wear a 'sports jacket' c.1930, while later, in 1940, my grandmother (previously a court dressmaker) removed my evacuee mother from her rural host family because she was being dressed in another child's clothes. Vivid dress-related memories and family stories are part of oral history and never far from our consciousness. Some of us are also fortunate to possess more tangible souvenirs in the form of photographs and paintings, inherited clothes, jewellery and printed or hand-written documents. Some of these relics, especially faded garments and personal jewellery powerfully evoke the presence of their former owners.

Fashion reflects the wider world, yet it is also intensely private: on a personal level, choosing garments and accessories; shopping and visiting markets; manufacturing or selling cloth; making, mending and laundering clothes … these and countless related activities helped to shape the daily routines of past generations. Dress and clothing are firmly enmeshed in ordinary human experience and exploring these areas of the past illuminates family history in fascinating and thought-provoking ways.

My Auntie, a Metal Box Factory London worker, wearing a fashionable Surrealist-inspired hat in 1938.

Chapter 1

Fashion Timeline, 1800–1950

It seems apt to begin this book by taking a traditional approach, tracing the chronological development of mainstream fashion throughout the period. This aims to create an ordered historical framework for our subject and offer a firm foundation for more advanced exploration of our ancestors' relationship with clothes. The stylistic timeline below demonstrates the evolution of dress as a continuing process, the illustrations presenting sequential historical images in context also providing clear visual examples to aid comparison and dating of family artworks and photographs.

A brief note on the pictures in this chapter and throughout the book: all integrated black and white images and the separate colour plates are firmly dated, or closely dateable, providing explicit historical reference material. When considering a broad time span, as here, the nature of pictorial sources shifts, becoming more plentiful and diverse over time. Therefore images displaying early- to mid-nineteenth century styles are typically prints, sketches or fashion plates, while from the mid-1800s onwards photographic portraits come into play. Genuine family photographs are featured wherever possible, occasionally augmented by artworks or advertisements to enhance the visual sequence.

As demonstrated below, male and female fashions have generally been shaped by the same aesthetic principles, inspiring a corresponding silhouette at any given time: for instance slender and elongated, or full and broad. Numerous dress terms were used over time, their exact contemporary meaning not always clear today, so to avoid complications this study uses the most common or generic names. As we shall see, during the early to mid-1800s, men's and women's clothes increasingly diverged, male garments growing more sombre and standardised, women's appearing comparatively decorative, more diverse. From the late-nineteenth century, everyday female fashion grew more functional, emulating aspects of menswear, the twentieth century eventually ushering in more natural, modern forms.

Women's Styles

In 1800 the neo-classical taste established in the late 1700s inspired fashion, dictating a columnar line and loosely draped effects emulating antique statuary. Simple *chemise* gowns were styled with a high waistline, set below the bust, the length falling in vertical folds to the ground, hemlines trained at the back for formal dress. Gown necklines were low, and by day a modest insert, half-blouse (*chemisette*) or kerchief covered the chest; sleeves were elbow-length or long. Plain-coloured and printed cotton materials were popular for ordinary wear, finer garments fashioned from diaphanous light-coloured or white muslin sprigged with delicate embroidery. While

Fashion plate from *Heideloff's Gallery of Fashion*, 1801.

ornamentation was discreet, coloured ribbon trimmings, fitted gloves, flat leather or fabric boots or pumps, picturesque bonnets, muffs and long reticule bags were fashionable accessories. Hair was short-medium length, often layered and casually tousled or arranged in natural-looking curls secured with combs, classical-style bandeaux or turban headdresses. A long Indian shawl added interest, and for extra warmth a short coloured spencer jacket or slender pelisse coat were worn outdoors.

The pure neo-classical line began to disperse around the mid-1810s, as diverse influences affected dress. Sturdier fabrics replaced sheer muslins and shorter, ankle-length hemlines were stiffened and padded, creating more structured garments. Interest in past modes prompted decorative puffed sleeves and 'historical' ruff-like necklines, hair more rigidly styled with centre-parting and high sausage curls. Diverse headwear included turban-like caps, straw 'country' bonnets and military-inspired *casquettes*, reflecting the recent Napoleonic Wars (1803–1815); shawls, large fur muffs and stoles ('tippets') fashionable accessories. These picturesque trends continued into the 1820s when advancing Romantic taste favoured more prominent ornamentation, bold, dramatic colours and rich materials. The high waistline, having steadily lowered since the late 1810s, regained natural waist level by c.1825.

An exaggerated hourglass silhouette evolved in the mid- to late 1820s, comprising a tight-fitting bodice and tightly corseted waist accentuated with a prominent buckled belt. Full ankle-length skirts were counterbalanced by ballooning *gigot* sleeves, wide-collared outdoor coats emphasising the artificial line. Extreme hairstyles displayed nodding sausage curls at the temples and tall arrangements of looped, plaited and knotted hair gummed into striking coiffures such as the 'Apollo knot'. Hats also grew larger, piled with feathers, flowers and bows, completing the artificial effect that dominated fashion until the mid-1830s.

During the later 1830s, the extravagant look diminished, the shoulder-line dropping and buoyant upper sleeves deflating, gaining discreet flounces, gathers and bows on the lower arm. Separate pelerines or shoulder capes grew fashionable, while skirts widened further, supported by several underskirts and horsehair petticoats. A pointed bodice front developed, becoming increasingly pronounced. High chignons lowered, centrally parted hair now dressed into low side ringlets, or draped over the ears. Shawls remained fashionable, parasols also admired, and bonnets grew tall and oval, completing the dainty, feminine look associated with the beginning of Queen Victoria's reign.

In the early to mid-1840s a tight, constricted silhouette developed, reflecting the Gothic Revival taste for narrow arches and angles. Fashionable dress comprised a rigid, figure-hugging bodice, shaped with darts and seams to form a pointed V-shaped centre-front, attached to a full, dome-shaped skirt. Sleeves were exceedingly narrow, a round or V-shaped neckline set off by a deep lace collar or *pelerine*. Plain or 'changeable' ('shot') silks in muted

Fashion plate from *The Ladies' Pocket Magazine*, 1836.

colours or modest checked materials were fashionable for formal daywear, an enveloping cloak or loose coat worn outdoors. Hair was centrally parted, continuing the fashion for low ringlets, plaits or coils around the ears. Bonnets were narrow, shielding the face and accentuating the meek, demure early-Victorian image.

From the late 1840s an easier line evolved: softly pleated bodice *bretelles* converged from shoulders to centre-front, waistlines growing more natural and rounded. Short jacket-bodices were a novel fashion, full skirts often flounced in tiers, creating an illusion of width, until in 1856/57 the new cage crinoline

Ambrotype photograph, early 1850s.

frame was introduced: an under-structure formed of widening concentric hoops that produced a vast circular skirt. Sleeves became looser, opening at the wrists, the 'pagoda' shape dominating the 1850s, culminating in an extremely wide 'hanging pagoda' sleeve. White under-sleeves (*engageantes*) were usually worn beneath, their lace or *broderie anglaise* decoration echoing that of the neat white collar at the neck. Hair remained centrally parted, draped down, Madonna-like, over the ears, the length secured behind in a low chignon. Neat circular bonnets framed the face and shawls, mantles and cloaks sat well with the vast skirt.

The 1860s opened with bulky costumes displaying vast swaying crinoline skirts, the bodice plain or pleated, and open pagoda sleeves continuing until c.1862, after when the dominant shape was a closed 'bishop' sleeve. Silks and mixed materials in newly developed bright aniline (artificial) colours such as purple, azure blue, emerald green and mustard yellow were fashionable for formal wear, accentuating the conspicuous effect. A short bolero-type jacket, the *zouave*, worn with coordinating skirt was an early 1860s' trend, many garments displaying contrasting bands of braid on the sleeve and around the hem. Short, wide *paletot* jackets comprised fashionable outerwear, teamed with an oval bonnet or small, round 'pork pie' hat. Hair was draped low over, or just behind, the ears, the length sometimes contained behind the neck in a hair net or *caul*.

By around mid-decade, formal gowns appeared slimmer; use of the circular crinoline frame declined, narrower skirts now shaped with gores, a more slender waistline accentuated with a fabric belt. Increasingly the skirt front flattened, with fashionable emphasis centred on the back, while bodices of the mid- to late 1860s gained epaulette-style shoulder features or square yokes. Simultaneously hairstyles rose higher, tresses drawn well off the face, revealing the ears and neck, and inspiring a vogue for long pendant earrings. Older ladies still favoured capacious shawls and bonnets, while younger style-conscious women wore loose 'dolman-style' jackets and neat hats.

Cdv photograph, c.1869–70.

As the fashionable line developed, eventually the ample back drapery required support: a modest half-crinoline or *crinolette* evolved by c.1869/70 into a more substantial projecting 'dress improver', 'bustle' or *tournure* (polite French term) behind the waist. An exuberant, soft, feminine look now dominated the early to mid-1870s. Fashionable costumes all featured double skirts, an extended bodice or overdress typically draped up *polonaise*-style, the swathes and prominent back drapery creating a padded, bouffant effect, the lower skirt floor length or trained. Ornate bodices were variously styled with open or closed sleeves, high necklines with frill, bow or cravat/necktie (*jabot*), or alternatively lace-edged V-shaped or square necklines set off by ribbon chokers. Hairstyles were also elaborate, extreme chignons arranged as a heavy mass behind the head or wound into plaited coils while releasing long tresses or ringlets on to the shoulders. Jaunty hats were tilted forward, 'postilion' style, over the intricate coiffure.

In 1874/75 fashion dictated another stylistic shift, underpinned by a new, rigid *cuirass* corset that moulded the torso and hips in a continuous line, effectively forcing the early 1870s' bustle downwards. A slimmer silhouette emerged from mid-decade onwards, costumes now characterised by lengthening bodices and narrowing skirts, the skirt material drawn or gathered closely across the front, residual back drapery cascading into a train. Fabric bows ornamented the horizontal gathers and hemlines were often edged with dainty knife-edge pleats. All dress was tight-fitting, with narrow sleeves; notable garment styles of the era were a front-buttoning one-piece 'princess' dress, and, by contrast, a plain tailored costume comprising hip-length jacket-bodice and skirt that emulated the male suit. Hairstyles became smoother and lowered in height, ultra-fashionable young women favouring a short fringe of front hair. Headwear – both hats and bonnets – became raised in front, following the new vertical silhouette.

Cdv photograph, c.1878–80.

The slender lines of late 1870s' fashion grew more extreme during the early 1880s, modern costumes appearing tight and sheath-like. Long trains were discontinued by day, narrow skirts now worn well off the ground, the hem often resting on the shoe. Stronger, richer colours such as wine red, russet, chocolate brown and dark purple were admired, along with contrasting fabrics, for instance woollen cloth juxtaposed with panels of satin, velvet or plush (cotton velvet). Garments were further ornamented with complex bands of decoration – gathers, ruches, shirring and rows of pleats. Figure-hugging bodices fastened tightly down the front with tiny buttons and displayed exceedingly narrow sleeves, often shortened above the wrist. High necklines were accessorised with a circular lace collar and/or chunky gold chain suspending large pendant or locket. Slender three-quarter pelisse coats followed the narrow lines of dress and bonnets, hats and soft toques (brimless hats) featured low crowns.

By c.1882/83 the vertical silhouette was breaking up again, as the narrow skirt gained additional fabric around the hips arranged as horizontal drapery or in pouch-like side *paniers*. Minor stylistic variations characterised this transitional period, but by 1884/85 a new line was fully established, the skirt front draped 'apron'-style over a pleated or plain under-skirt, the back raised up over another bustle or *tournure*. This second bustle was sharper, more pronounced than the first and often projected deeply c.1886–88: usually a lightweight, collapsible under-structure, it was sometimes observed wobbling around as the wearer moved.

Fashionable bodices remained tight-fitting and acquired a very high, close collar, the sleeves exceedingly narrow. The centre-front also grew pointed, the severe effect accentuated by the continuation of plain dark materials, including the use of functional fabrics like serge (robust twilled woollen or worsted material). Often the late 1880s' bodice was styled with mock lapels or a 'waistcoat' effect, the fashionable *plastron* front featuring the contrasting fabric inserts that remained in vogue. Indeed, late 1880s' dress could appear very majestic when velvet, plush, satin and fashionable trimmings were used. Hair was sometimes cut short around the face, a soft fringe highly fashionable, sleeker styles being dressed into a high coil or chignon. Cape-like dolman jackets with wide sleeves or arm slits complemented the 1880s' bustle and between 1885/56 and 1890 tall headwear dominated fashion.

By c.1889 the skirt bustle projection was diminishing although some ladies continued to use modest padding around the hips. During the early 1890s, bodices remained tight, the centre-front still sharply pointed and neckline high, while fashionable sleeves began to be gathered, displaying modest vertical shoulder puffs. Cloth for daywear was often sombre and short, tailored jackets worn over a blouse grew fashionable. Hair was unremarkable, dressed close to the head in a smooth chignon. Accessories included a neat straw or felt hat with moderate brim, fitted leather gloves, an umbrella/parasol and handbag.

Cdv photograph, c.1886–88.

Jewellery was discreet, a narrow horizontal bar brooch at the neck replacing the circular brooches of the 1880s. Increasing numbers of women now wore a watch and chain attached to their clothes.

The onward trend in the 1890s was for a more curvaceous hourglass silhouette, reflecting the emergence of *Art Nouveau*, the sinuous *fin-de-siècle* aesthetic style. A natural waistline developed by mid-decade, the cinched waist accentuated by padded hips, prominent belt or waistband, while gored skirts flared gracefully outwards to the floor. Simultaneously, the modest early 1890s' sleeve puff steadily expanded, reaching maximum width in 1895/56, when vast, balloon-like *gigot* or 'leg-o'-mutton' sleeves were matched by wide shoulders – a style prompting a vogue for shoulder capes. Dressy daytime costumes featured brighter silks and satin materials and ornate patterned, lace- or ribbon-trimmed bodices. Hairstyles grew softer, fuller, the length lightly frizzed and drawn loosely off the face, fashionable coiffures balancing plate-like hats ornamented with feathers, flowers and bows. During the late 1890s, sleeve puffs gradually diminished, withdrawing up the arm, forming a neat puffball, frill or epaulette c.1898–1900. Although formal 1890s' fashions appeared extravagant, for daywear separate blouses, skirts and jackets were increasingly popular: the smart, functional 'tailor-made' costume resembled the male suit and epitomised the so-called 'New Woman' at the turn of the century.

The early 1900s continued the shapely hourglass silhouette; even functional garments were underpinned by the so-called 'S-bend' corset that pushed back the hips, thrusting the bosom forwards. High-necked bodices and blouses featured floating panels and full fronts to emphasise the bust, while formal variants were much-embellished with ornamental frills, lace bands, inserts and rows of vertical tucks. Sleeves, predominantly narrow in 1900, flared out towards the wrist and gathered into a cuff c.1901–05. Skirts

Snapshot photograph, dated October 1898.

were relatively plain, still tailored with shaped panels, wide hemlines edged with flounces that, along with swishing under-petticoats, produced the fashionable Edwardian 'frou frou' effect. Hairstyles remained soft and full, drawn up loosely into a high bun, the small 'cottage loaf' knot a popular style. Formal hats with moderate brims were worn straight or upturned, and ornamented with feathers, net and flowers. Outdoors, women wore tailored jackets or longer coats: for everyday wear men's headwear might be appropriated: flat woollen caps or the summer straw boater.

Garment types changed little throughout the early 1900s; a one-piece dress usual for formal wear, blouse, skirt and jacket increasingly common for daywear, with changes of blouse for different events. Decorative versions featured high choker-like collars, the plain 'shirt-waist' often worn with masculine collar and neck tie. Fashionable sleeve shapes evolved c.1905, gaining fullness from shoulder to just below the elbow; there began a deep fitted cuff, or the sleeve ended, edged with

Snapshot photograph, dated 1904.

pronounced frill or flounce. Hair and hat styles also changed around mid-decade; hair, still thick and long either raised over pads or false pieces into a full, upswept style, or centrally parted and styled into two wide swathes above the temples. Fashionable headwear c.1906–10 favoured a wide-brimmed hat with similarly broad crown; trimmed with flowers and ribbons, these styles resembled vast decorated gateaux.

From c.1908/09 a new silhouette began to emerge, initially launched in Paris as the revived neo-classical *Directoire* line, reflecting its slightly high waist and slender form. Eschewing extreme artificial corsetry, this was a more natural style – a development now regarded as representing the start of modern fashion. One-piece dresses with fitted elbow-length sleeves were layered over a high-necked blouse, *chemisette*, or incorporated a bodice insert. Skirts might be draped asymmetrically, tunic-like, and c.1911–14 fashion-conscious ladies adopted the exaggerated 'hobble' skirt that hugged the legs and ankles. Tailored suits, ever popular, also reflected the narrower silhouette, gaining longer jackets and slimmer skirts, with hemlines rising from floor-length to ankle-length during the early 1910s. High Edwardian necklines remained in vogue until c.1913, but informal blouses now featured lower, rounded necklines. In general, fashion was sleeker, smoother and less cluttered than previously; discreet, two-dimensional embroidery and appliqué work favoured over traditional frills and flounces. Vast 'Titanic-era' hats grew enormous brims c.1910–13, their sweeping lines often set off by a stylish statement flower or single plume.

The Great War, later called the First World War (1914–1918), was underway when fashion decreed another major shift in women's dress. From late 1914 and during 1915, narrow, ankle-length skirts rose to mid-calf level and hemlines grew wider, forming the so-called 'war crinoline' that gave greater

Postcard photograph, dated August 1914.

physical freedom to millions of working women. By 1914/1
blouses were front-buttoning, a quick, convenient fastening that enabled
efficient dressing, unaided. The flared skirt, front-buttoned collared
shirt and loosely belted jacket became a virtual wartime 'uniform',
teamed with laced leather boots and neat felt hat. In around 1917, hats
developed wide skimming brims and jacket/blouse collars grew large
reveres – long and narrow or broad, extending over the shoulders, sailor
fashion. Substantial one-piece garments known as 'coat dresses' or 'coat
frocks' in serviceable fabrics featured useful outside pockets. Loose-
belted cardigans became popular and, in general, comfortable knitwear
(previously worn mainly for sports: see Chapter 6) entered the regular
wardrobe.

Between c.1918 and 1922, a billowing 'barrel-shape' was the prevailing
line, the hems of suits, frocks and coat dresses set around mid-calf. The
customary large-collared wartime blouse remained popular, while new
trends included soft crocheted or knitted tops drawn in at the waist
with loose ties or pompom fastenings. Often home-made, these worked
well with squashy toque or 'Tam-o'-shanter' hats and other knitwear,
while more tailored outerwear developed cape-like shoulder features
or fashionable fur collars. Low-cut shoes having become a fashionable
alternative to boots during the war, bar shoes became widely established
c.1922/23. Many war workers had bobbed their hair and afterwards
more women adopted the daring look, others compromising by cutting
front hair and styling 'kiss curls' on the cheek, the length pinned back
into a bun. By mid-decade, most fashionable women were wearing soft
bobbed haircuts and this encouraged adoption of close-fitting, helmet-
style hats.

As the 1920s advanced, garments grew simple in cut: plain blouses,
jackets and skirts continued, but straight, loose dresses predominated.
Collars grew outmoded and plainer round or scooped necklines
encouraged the wearing of strings of pearls or beads at the neck – an
iconic 1920s' accessory. Sleeves of frocks were often elbow-length, and
calf-length hemlines prevailed until garments grew significantly shorter,
rising to knee-length from 1925. For the first time in history, the entire
lower leg and foot were displayed, encouraging natural flesh-coloured
stockings. During the later 1920s, synthetic fabrics improved, notably
silk substitutes. Whether natural silk, cotton, linen, wool, or the new
artificial silk ('art silk': rayon), fabric designs included bold stripes,
squares and artistic abstract motifs, reflecting the prevailing *Art Deco*

Postcard photograph, late 1920s.

aesthetic. Single- or double-bar shoes were common footwear, and fitted cloche hats, worn low over the forehead, the prevailing headwear from 1925. From mid-decade, many women favoured comfortable sweater suits in soft jersey fabric, acceptable for most daytime occasions. Some bold women favoured an extreme 'garçon' look that rejected all feminine curves, pioneering tubular shift-like clothes and boyish cropped hair, while wearing cosmetics and giving rise to the racy 'flapper' image of the mid- to late 1920s.

By c.1930, minimalist modes were softening, skirts and frocks growing fuller and uneven 'handkerchief' hemlines briefly in vogue. During the early to mid-1930s, garment hemlines were generally set at mid-low calf-length and flowing, draped fabrics – plain, chevron-patterned or floral printed – created the fashionable fluid line. Feminine blouses were revived, some featuring long tie necklines or Peter Pan collars and often teamed with knitted sweaters and cardigans. Fashionable hairstyles were cut to around chin length, and softly waved, while neat hats included versions of the close-fitting cloche, angled berets and pull-on 'beanies'; wide-brimmed picture hats, admired for formal summer wear. During the early 1930s, bar shoes gave way to plainer court shoes with elegant heels; coordinating handbags and gloves completed the ladylike outfit.

From c.1935/36 a crisper, more tailored look evolved, the new style well-established by the outbreak of war in 1939. Garments gained stiff padded shoulders, blouse and frock sleeves often puffed. Hemlines grew shorter again, set just below the knee, and smart checks and plain fabrics were fashionable for daytime suits. Fur collars, stoles and shoulder capes were widely worn, jackets and outer coats sharply styled. Hats of the later 1930s were also more structured, often asymmetrical or worn at an angle, some headwear quirkily surrealist in form. Hair was generally grown longer, to around collar length. A few women were starting to wear tailored slacks for sports and leisure wear (see Chapters 5 & 6) pre-empting future trends.

Snapshot photograph, dated 1943.

The Second World War (1939–1945) and its aftermath dominated dress during the 1940s. Styles continued along late 1930s' tailored lines, but British civilian fashion took a back seat, evolving along a unique path, reflecting the exigencies of war. Ordinary garments were rationed between 1941 and 1949 and the Utility clothing scheme of 1942–52 restricted quantities of fabric and trimmings (including pockets and buttons), inspiring an economical, trim silhouette. Dresses and skirts were short, knee-length, slightly A-line in shape, plain or featuring modest pleats. Fitted bodices and blouses bore little decoration, but puffed sleeves, draped cowl necklines or ruching added interest. Dresses and outer clothes usually had square padded shoulders and gained a smart, uniform-like look.

Some women wore trousers during the war: dungarees, breeches, slacks or jodhpurs. This sparked a new trend and, along with growing American fashion influence, relaxed separates grew popular. Workaday wartime footwear usually comprised a sensible low-heeled laced leather shoe, or substantial summer sandals; more elegant court shoes kept for smarter wear. Collar- or shoulder-length hair was curled, waved or rolled off the face during the 1940s, presenting a feminine, glamorous image. When Christian Dior's controversial 'New Look', favouring soft curves and using yards of precious fabric, was launched in 1947, it met with enthusiasm from women desiring a more feminine image after the years of austerity dress. Many clothes were influenced by the New Look throughout the late 1940s and 1950s.

Men's Dress

Men's appearance in the early 1800s expressed prevailing neo-classical taste through moulded garments that outlined bodily contours, rather like antique statuary. Expertly tailored clothes of immaculate fit shaped the admired silhouette; a plain, close-fitting tail coat with cutaway fronts and slender pale-coloured breeches or longer calf-/ankle-length pantaloons, worn with tall fitted boots or shoes. This elegant ensemble was accessorised with fine linen neckwear and a long 'bicorne' or round black hat, hair cropped, layered and swept forward à la Titus or à la Brutus, referencing imperial Rome. Dominating fashion for the first fifteen to twenty years of the nineteenth century, this impeccable look typified the Regency 'dandy'.

Subtle garment variations reflected different occasions or looks; formal dress tail coats were cut straight across at the waist, while more relaxed frock, morning or riding coats featured sloping front edges. Both were crisply tailored in black or dark green, brown, claret and navy cloth – a perfect foil for the white linen shirt with starched collar resting on the jawline and expertly arranged white cravat. Cream or light buff-coloured breeches or pantaloons accentuated a shapely thigh and calf. Seals were suspended from the waist, a black beaver hat, boots or white stockings and flat buckled shoes completing the late-Georgian image. For riding and

Fashion plate from *Le Beau Monde*, April 1808

fashionable outdoor wear swallow-tailed riding coats, breeches, tasselled 'hussar', 'hessian' or black leather boots with brown tops ('top boots', as worn by grooms and jockeys), leather gloves and a hard-crowned riding hat expressed the country sporting strand of fashion. This dashing yet unpretentious, quintessentially English style, was admired throughout Europe as reassuringly 'democratic' in the aftermath of the French Revolution.

From the mid-1810s onwards, as the sculpted neo-classical style began to decline, dress diverged, including a notable development the vogue for ankle-length 'trowsers' (to use their original spelling), previously worn mainly at sea. After a transitional, experimental period, by the mid-1820s long trousers teamed with shoes or short half-boots rivalled traditional pantaloons and breeches for daywear, worn with a new style frock coat – a substantial knee-length garment with straight front edges. While functional trousers became more firmly established for daywear, Romantic-inspired frock coats of the later 1820s and 1830s were artificially padded at the shoulders and chest, producing an exaggerated hourglass silhouette to mirror female modes. Smaller dress items like waistcoats and neckwear also grew more pronounced, the waistcoat often brightly coloured or patterned at this time. Hair was also worn longer, tousled or curly, while bushy sideburns added to the rugged image. A round black hat with rising crown was emerging as the prototype of the Victorian top hat, while caped greatcoats continued outdoors – or cloaks, for a romantic flourish.

Menswear grew more restrained from the late 1830s under the young Queen Victoria, although the trend towards sobriety was already underway. Notwithstanding the bold waistcoats and cravats still favoured by some, mainstream male dress was becoming a sober, industrial-age city 'uniform' and for the next twenty years followed a slim, Gothic line. The formal tail coat persisted, but more common was the fitted, dark, knee-length frock coat – or its summer variant, a lightweight duster coat – tailored

Watercolour painting, c.mid-1830s.

with narrow, elongated sleeves. Trousers were also of slender cut, the addition of braces and under-foot straps ensuring a smooth fit. Waistcoats, patterned or plain, sometimes incorporated a breast pocket for a pocket watch and chain, a popular timepiece the new 'Albert' watch. The top hat now became firmly established for formal business and smart daywear, a tall-crowned 'stovepipe' hat accentuating the vertical silhouette.

From the late 1850s, fashionable male dress acquired a wider cut and simultaneously new informal garments began to evolve, notably easy-fitting short, casual overcoats, capes and lightweight jackets broadly termed the 'paletot'. The 'lounging' jacket, a loose thigh-length garment initially designed for the seaside, country wear and spectator sports, also became a staple of the modern wardrobe. Complementing the bulkier garments emerging, top hats lowered and new semi-casual hat styles entered the scene, including the wide-brimmed 'wide-awake', the felt 'billycock', straw summer hats, the round 'muffin hat' and various peaked caps. Hair was often parted and worn longish on top, causing side curls to jut out at ear level; meanwhile soldiers returning from the Crimean War (1853–1856) reportedly encouraged the new fashion for beards. The 1850s/early 1860s' beard was generally grown down from the sideburns underneath the chin – a distinctive mid-century innovation.

For much of the 1860s, clothes remained easy-fitting, the lounge jacket with useful outside pockets gaining acceptance for semi-formal daywear, typically teamed with contrasting trousers. The mid-Victorian morning coat, also cut generously, was smarter, often of heavier cloth and when worn with dark trousers and waistcoat comprised a formal business suit. Early in the decade, trousers were often of the peg-top variety, wide at the waist and tapering towards the ankles, but from the later 1860s, all clothes narrowed again, the suit gaining an increasingly streamlined, businesslike look. Ornate waistcoats and cravats were shunned and extra starch was used on shirts, accentuating the stiff crispness of

Ambrotype photograph, mid- to late 1850s.

collars and cuffs; even hair began to be cut shorter. The middle-class businessman avoided extreme modes; with prominent watch chain, full beard and top hat creating an air of masculinity and authority, the mid-Victorian male looked sober-suited and industrious.

Men were expected to dress appropriately for their position, the occasion and time of day, and as new garments proliferated, so the usage of existing items shifted. Significantly, the lounge jacket, initially considered casual wear, came to form part of a coordinated three-piece suit (or suit of 'dittos', as it was called) – the prototype of the modern lounge or business suit. During the late 1860s to the mid-1870s, both the lounge jacket and sloping morning coat featured wide, curved lapels sometimes faced with contrasting velvet cloth. Accessorised with a turned-down shirt collar and broad 'four-in-hand' knotted tie or wide cravat, this versatile suit gained popularity, becoming the 'Sunday best' of the working man, and casual wear for those higher up the social scale. The stately frock coat was less fashionable, but still favoured by the conservative middle- and upper-classes, teamed with formal top hat. However, the round-crowned bowler hat, fashionable from c.1860, became a firm favourite throughout the 1870s. Facial hair was pronounced and various beard styles were popular, from long, full beards, to bushy 'mutton-chop' whiskers. Outerwear also advanced, a range of overcoats in warm woollen materials now available, including the caped Ulster and Inverness – sturdy styles ideal for travelling.

During the late 1870s and 1880s, the silhouette grew increasingly slender; morning coats and suit jackets became closer-fitting with neat, high-fastening lapels, the jacket edges, collars and cuffs often bound with smart silk braid. A white handkerchief in the top jacket pocket became established during the 1880s as a gentlemanly accessory. Neckwear included a pinned silk cravat and newly fashionable bow tie fastened below a standing shirt collar. As trousers narrowed

Cdv photograph, 1870s.

throughout the 1880s, their slender line was accentuated by stripes, a black morning coat and elegant grey pin-striped trousers now archetypal business and general semi-formal wear. Echoing the tall proportions of ladies' headwear, from the mid-1880s bowler crowns also rose high, emphasising the vertical line. Some young men-about-town adopted extreme versions of such fashions, carrying ornamental canes, oiling their hair and cultivating a slick moustache.

Alternative late-Victorian modes were the short black or navy double-breasted 'pilot coat' and nautical-inspired 'reefer' jacket – more relaxed fashions popular with younger men, workers, and for holidays and leisure wear. As the 1890s advanced, the fit

Cdv photograph c.1888–92.

of all clothes eased slightly, the coordinating three-piece tailored suit now widely worn throughout society. The new trouser press facilitated centre-front and back trouser creases, while jacket and coat necklines lowered, revealing waistcoats again. Shirts sparkled with starch and gained high standing collars, neckwear ranging from cravats and narrow bow ties to modern long knotted ties. Bushy beards were outmoded, yet retained by some older, conservative males and outdoor workers. More fashionable was a close-clipped beard resembling that worn by the Prince of Wales (later Edward VII). New bowler hats featured a moderate crown, remaining customary for respectable daywear. Summer headwear included straw boaters and other wide-brimmed straw hats, the round woollen cloth cap – formerly worn by sportsmen – now entering mainstream fashion and becoming the badge of the late-Victorian working man.

Early in the new century, the elegant morning suit was generally favoured for city business and formal daywear, the respectable three-piece lounge suit widely worn for work and 'Sunday best'. Clothes were of moderate, comfortable cut, jacket lapels short; formal starched shirt collars stood high until c.1903/04, the stiff turned-down collar

Postcard photograph dated 1910.

with rounded points subsequently prevalent, usually accessorised with the long knotted tie. Older men still wore beards, generally clipped in the pointed style favoured by the new King, Edward VII. Middle-aged men tended to favour a moustache, the young generation preferring the modern clean-shaven look.

The male silhouette began to shift during the late-Edwardian era, echoing female modes. An elongated line was expressed in long, thigh-length suit jackets with thin lapels and narrow cropped trousers revealing leather boots. Bowler hats remained current, but new semi-formal styles were developing, namely the homburg and trilby-style felt hats with dented crown. The working man's cloth cap was most popular, the shape flattening and widening during the 1910s. Naturally, many men wore military uniforms during the First World War and civilian modes in 1919 resembled pre-war styles. However, several new trends had emerged during the war and would soon become established: soft-collared shirts were now common; low-cut laced shoes were replacing traditional boots and convenient wrist watches were beginning to supersede the old fashioned watch and chain.

During the 1920s, as popular culture – music, dance and film – influenced dress, youthful fashions included slicked-down Rudolph Valentino hairstyles, tilted gangster-style trilby hats and, from mid-decade, wide 'Oxford bags' trousers with exaggerated turn-ups. Yet the respectable mode for work and many social occasions was the tailored three-piece suit. Narrow knotted neckties were customary 1920s' daywear, winged collars and bow ties a more 'dressy' or stylish option. Bowler hats were growing old-fashioned, used mainly for business; most men preferred felt trilby or fedora-style hats or the ubiquitous cloth cap, still flat and wide; summer straw Panama hats superseded the traditional boater.

'Walking picture' postcard, early to mid–1930s.

Men's garments were growing wider by 1930, setting a new trend for the next twenty or more years. 1930s' suits were boxy in style, jackets often double-breasted, fashioned with wide padded shoulders and sharp lapels. Trousers were generously cut, worn loose and shapeless on weekends, with smart creases and turn-ups for work and formal wear. Neckties grew broader, encouraging stripes, repeating motifs and other patterned effects. Tailored waistcoats remained current, but with knitwear becoming firmly established in the wardrobe (see Chapters 5 & 8) in certain workplaces and for casual wear some men wore a knitted jersey or sleeveless vest ('slip-over') instead, or went without. Ties were also beginning to be discontinued for weekend wear, a wide open-collared effect typical of the decade.

War broke out again in 1939 and with many men in uniform for the next six or seven years, fashion took a back seat. Civilian males continued to wear their pre-war clothes, a tailored suit with shirt and tie remaining the convention in many jobs. Men's new clothing was subject to rationing and utility guidelines: single-breasted jackets replaced double-breasted, lapel size and number of pockets were restricted; similarly, less material was to be used in the tailoring of trousers and turn-ups were eliminated. The abolition of turn-ups was particularly unpopular, leading some to buy their trousers too long and have them altered at home. Upon discharge in

1945/46, servicemen received a standardised, shapeless 'demob' suit by way of a basic outfit, designed to equip them for their return to civilian life. Only after clothes rationing ended in 1949 was there a major revival of interest in male fashion.

Children's Clothes

Historically, children's dress partly reflected adult modes, also following its own distinct path, expressing prevailing ideas about childhood. Babywear was considered special, the precise age at which infants wore particular garments shifting over time, and varying according to family circumstances. Once out of baby clothes, in general girls and boys were clothed in styles deemed appropriate for their age as they progressed through childhood and adolescence. In fashionable, comfortably placed families there could be many subtle gradations in children's attire, whereas in poorer homes there were fewer clothes and children were dressed in the best available.

(i) Babywear

In 1800, the traditional practice of swaddling babies prevailed, traditional thinking being that young babies might catch cold or hurt themselves if allowed unrestrained movement. As Clare Rose explains in *Children's Clothes*, first baby was dressed in a linen shirt open down front or back, then a long 'bellyband' of sturdy fabric wrapped around the body to flatten the navel and support the lower back and stomach. The napkin was a square of linen fabric, then came one or two linen caps, sometimes with an extra triangular forehead piece for warmth and decoration. Swaddling clothes themselves comprised a large rectangular 'bed' that wrapped around the body, containing the arms at the sides, turned up at the feet and pinned in place. Sometimes another 'bed' was arranged on top, the final article the 'stayband', a linen strip laid under the cap and pinned to the clothes at shoulder height to keep the head straight. Despite growing condemnation, swaddling continued for at least another generation: deemed beneficial to health, inevitably it also had a calming effect and in poorer families the restraint of new-borns suited women with many chores to attend to.

At about 2–4 months old, the outer swaddling was removed and babies were put into an under-shirt, petticoats and long gown on top. Usually called a 'slip' dress and made of fine cambric, muslin or sturdier linen or cotton, this was of simple tucked construction and could be lengthened as the baby grew. Following simple neo-classical fashions, during the early 1800s, baby and toddler gowns for both sexes were white, lightweight and high-waisted, fashioned with short or elbow-length sleeves. Luxury garments and baby caps featured insertions of fine lace and net, and by 1820 baby clothes were growing more ornamental and picturesque, echoing fashionable Romantic tastes. In general, however, early-nineteenth-century babywear was skimpy, with extremely low necklines; consequently tie-on sleeves, shawls and capes were used outdoors.

By the Victorian era, the main remnant of the swaddling tradition was the 'binder' or 'roller' – a strip of flannel or robust cotton 3–4 inches wide

Fashion plate from *Ackermann's Repository of Arts*, January 1810.

wound repeatedly around the infant's body. Small babies of both sexes then wore several cotton petticoats, a linen shift and quilted or corded stays, over which was layered a long gown with decorative 'robings' – triangular panels framing the front panel of the bodice. High-quality cotton or muslin gowns were ornamented with delicate Ayrshire white work embroidery on bodice and skirt; by the late 1850s and 1860s, bolder *broderie anglaise* ornamentation was popular for the front panels and edgings of baby gowns. Lower down society, infants wore plainer high-necked, long-sleeved printed cotton or flannel gowns – garments resembling the nightgowns of those in prosperous households.

Victorian babies usually wore close-fitting caps and, where affordable, long, luxurious outdoor cloaks of fine wool or cashmere. The middle-class publication, *Cassell's Household Guide*, launched in 1868, recommended making for new-borns: a linen shirt open down the back; a 'day-flannel' or 'blanket'; one or more cotton petticoats and long cotton day gown. Underneath was a square napkin of figured linen or cotton towelling, a flannel 'pilch' (outer nappy wrapping) and optional hand-knitted socks. It was now recognised that tiny babies needed extra warmth and authorities advocated a 'first sized' high-necked gown with long sleeves, like the nightgown. Afterwards babies might progress to a shorter, short-sleeved tucked-fronted gown. By the 1890s, absorbent fabrics like 'Turkish' or 'terry' towelling were available for napkins and a new mackintosh (waterproof) pilch. A novel style of baby gown also evolved – high-necked, full-sleeved and with a yoke featuring decorative shoulder trim: resembling the smock dress recently introduced for small girls, it was ornamented, baby-fashion, with pin tucks, lace insertions and embroidered flounces. Carrying cloaks or capes, used for baby's outdoor airing, were usually of white/cream wool flannel, serge or cashmere for winter, cambric or cotton for summer.

Late-Victorian and Edwardian babies wore some of the most extravagant, impractical clothing ever designed. Tiny boys and girls were decked out in white 'Sunday best' smock-like gowns ornamented with frills, flounces, embroidery and lace and wide 'halo' bonnets. Throughout and after the First World War, the conventional baby's layette retained the traditional flannel petticoats and, commonly, flannel or stiff linen binders, wrapped around baby's stomach from chest to hips. Time-honoured recommendations concerning the wearing of wool next to the skin persisted and infants were often dressed in little woollen vests, combinations and sleep suits. Yet, following wider fashion, the growing trend was for simpler garments. The old distinction between the 'long clothes' worn by new-borns and the second 'shortening' set lessened and increasingly baby gowns were made of intermediate length and roomy enough to accommodate the first year's growth. Early forms of the romper suit also began to develop c.1919 for older babies at the crawling stage.

Between the wars, many families became accustomed to giving babies a daily 'airing' in a perambulator. Pram covers and blankets hid the infant's lower half, so outdoor clothing now focused on the head and upper body. A new outfit, the 'pram set', comprised

Cabinet photograph, late 1890s.

a woollen or fabric matinée jacket or short, caped pelisse coat, accessorised with matching hat and leggings. Hand-knitted babywear was highly popular and during the later 1920s and 1930s the now-familiar colour concept of 'pink for a girl, blue for a boy' became established. Another modern trend was to differentiate between the sexes at an increasingly early age through the styling of clothes, a development that explains the decline of the old 'breeching' tradition when sons were aged about 3½ – 5 years old. By c.1920 male toddlers were often dressed in a combined blouse and shorts outfit called the 'Buster' suit, a style still popular in the 1940s.

Throughout the Second World War the principles of 'make-do and mend' were rigorously applied to babywear

Postcard photograph, c.1929–33,

(for more on wartime practices, see Chapter 8). Only forty coupons were allocated annually for each baby's needs under the clothes rationing scheme. Garments were sometimes made of strong, nylon-like silk parachute panels, periodically circulated among families. Due to the need to improvise, there was great interest in new styles and materials during the war and this would influence baby fashions of the 1950s and 1960s.

(ii) Girls

Throughout the 1800s and early 1900s daughters advanced from infantile garments, through juvenile styles adapted to accommodate their changing form throughout puberty and beyond. Although 21 was the age of majority, officially marking adulthood, broadly females came 'of age' socially and adopted womanly modes of dress between 14 and 18 years old, depending on the era, the individual and her family circumstances. Essentially a girl's 'coming of age' dress-wise was represented by her progression to firmly fitted, adult-style corsets, the lowering of adolescent calf-length hemlines to the floor and the dressing of long loose hair up into a neat bun (chignon). This traditional rite of passage prevailed until female fashion at large modernised during the 1910s, after which sartorial age-related variations grew less pronounced. In affluent households where offspring enjoyed a comfortable, extended childhood, adult modes were typically adopted later than in working-class families where daughters, albeit still children, might be dressed for adult life as young as 14.

As we have seen, neo-classical modes influenced clothing from babyhood during the early 1800s and, like infants, girls wore flimsy white cotton or linen frocks based on the high-waisted adult chemise gown. The low neckline often had a drawstring

Watercolour painting, dated 1820.

and this was sometimes ornamented with ribbons complementing a ribbon sash at the waist. Otherwise the style was plain, the length of sleeves – short or long – offering subtle variations. Superficially it was a democratic fashion, since girls of all classes could wear the simple dresses, but status was expressed in the grade of the material, the delicacy of embroidery and lace insertions and quality of accessories: caps, bonnets, shawls, cloaks and gloves.

During the 1810s, girls' dresses continued to follow slender lines but grew more decorative, some incorporating 'robings' (also used in infants' clothes) – narrow panels flanking the centre-front section of the skirt. Printed cotton fabrics became widely available and a girl's short-sleeved dress might be made of bright-coloured flower-sprigged cotton fabric. Often such garments had separate long sleeves and small matching shoulder cape to tie on in colder weather, short cloaks or spencer jackets being usual for outdoors. More ornate Romantic influences impacted on girls' clothing during the 1820s and early 1830s; wide, boat-like necklines developed, sleeves developed vast puffs and hemlines widened and shortened. Ankle-length drawers were now worn under the clothes, their frilled or lace-edged hems displayed beneath the dress. For outdoor warmth was the short spencer jacket, longer pelisse or more workaday shawl.

By the early-Victorian period, fashionable clothing for young girls emulated ladies' evening gowns, with their off-the-shoulder necklines, short sleeves and full skirts. Now white dresses of fine cambric were favoured mainly for special occasions, delicate ornamentation including frills, lace insertions and satin bows, ordinary garments usually fashioned from heavier cottons, cotton-mixes, or wool. Full skirts were often supported with stiffened petticoats for a dome-like effect, knee-length hemlines on young daughters revealing long drawers (or *pantalettes*). When bodices lengthened during the 1840s, soft stays/corsets were adopted, or whalebone strips were sewn into bodice linings, even for small girls. Older girls' dresses

Fashion plate detail from *Le Petit Courier des Dames*, 1841.

resembled adult garments more closely and featured longer sleeves, in place of infants' short puffed sleeves. Tartan material for garments, ribbon trimmings and sashes became especially popular from the 1840s, encouraged by the royal family's love of the Scottish Highlands.

Throughout the 1850s and early 1860s, the fashionable girls' bodice often featured pleats, echoing ladies' styles. Wide skirts were accentuated by tiered flounces and, after 1856/57 older girls' calf- or ankle-length skirts might be supported by a mini wire crinoline frame. Woollen undergarments (worn as well as cotton underclothes) included flannel vests and chemises, a red flannel petticoat often glimpsed under full skirts. Indoors, a protective pinafore was worn over the frock; when made with short sleeves this sometimes substituted completely for the frock, preserving good dresses for 'best'. The form of girls' garments also received more attention and various picturesque styles evolved, for example the 'Garibaldi' blouse, following adult fashions. Long hair, worn loose by young girls, was usually waved and drawn off the face with an Alice band during the mid-Victorian era. Short capes and loose paletot jackets accessorised with circular pork pie hats grew fashionable, the shawl and bonnet more workaday styles.

By 1870 there was a clear shift away from wide crinoline skirts, the new adult bustle fashion finding juvenile form in elaborate scalloped or polonaise-style tunic-dresses, layered over flounced skirts, with bows or prominent drapery behind the waist. From the later 1870s, following the elongated *cuirass* line, girls' garments also acquired a longer, slender style. Contrasting bands of cloth and trimming were admired, but colours and materials were growing more restrained. As garments narrowed further during the early 1880s, the tubular Princess dress ornamented with ruched panels and pleats was popular, complemented by new straight (uncurled) hair and a short, straight-cut fringe. As the bustle returned to adult dress from c.1883/84, daughters' garments grew more fitted. By the mid-1880s even 4-year-olds wore frocks with tight-fitting, narrow-sleeved bodices, the bustle detail suggested by a broad hip sash and protruding bow behind the waist. Older girls often wore adult-style apron-fronted skirts displaying the full bustle projection and all female children adopted the tall headwear of the mid- to late 1880s.

Cdv photograph, c.1860.

Following the late-Victorian tendency for females to emulate male styles and growing interest in separates, an alternative for small girls was a feminine version of the popular boys' sailor suit – an easy-to-wear outfit combining loose naval-style blouse with pleated skirt. From the early 1890s another significant innovation was the smock dress gathered on to a fitted yoke, the length of fabric falling freely from the chest, full sleeves following the fashionable 'leg-o'-mutton' style. Loose and comfortable, smocks were worn by small girls from all social backgrounds and fashioned in various materials, from functional serge to hand-embroidered garments for special occasions. Older girls wore more fitted versions of the smock, caught in at the waist, or the blouse and separate skirt then coming into vogue.

No. 4771. WALKING DRESS, 6 TO 8 AND 8 TO 10 YEARS.   No. 4772. MORNING COSTUME, 12 TO 14 AND 14 TO 16 YEARS.   No. 4773. WASHING DRESS, 4 TO 6 YEARS.   No. 4774. THE "BRIGHTON" COSTUME, 12 TO 14 AND 14 TO 16 YEARS.   No. 4775. CANVAS COSTUME, 4 TO 6 AND 6 TO 8 YEARS.

Illustration from *Mrs Leach's Children's and Young Ladies' Dressmaker*, 1886.

The smock remained a firm favourite in the early 1900s. A white, high-necked, full-sleeved smock, worn alone, could be ornamented with frills and flounces for 'Sunday best', plain workaday and school smocks often worn beneath a protective pinafore. Loose, sleeveless pinafore dresses complemented the full smock and remained a favourite for small girls until the First World War. As in the late-Victorian era, older girls wore a modified smock, the dress fabric fitted at the waist for a more mature effect, or the more modern blouse and calf-length tailored skirt. For winter, traditional black woollen stockings were worn with buttoned boots or

Cabinet photograph, mid to late 1890s.

modern laced footwear; for summer small girls often wore short white stockings (socks) with coloured or white leather shoes. Capes and caped coats were fashionable as outerwear, a wide-brimmed hat or picturesque bonnet completing the Edwardian girl's outfit.

Following wider fashion trends, during the 1910s juvenile clothes grew shorter and simpler in style. Initially loose smock dresses continued, but by mid-decade young girls generally wore slimmer-fitting frocks with waist seam and elbow-length sleeves. Edwardian frills and flounces were outmoded, although picturesque collars and *broderie anglaise* hemline trimmings were admired. Long hair was generally worn loose, or styled into ringlets, accessorised with one or two large white bows – an identifying

Postcard photograph, c.1919–21.

feature of this era. Older girls often favoured a blouse and skirt, hair tied into a ponytail with large black bow. This was also the period when recognisable school uniform developed, young schoolgirls wearing a blouse and pinafore-style gymslip, older pupils a tailored blazer/jacket with matching calf-length skirt, shirt waist blouse and knotted tie. School colours helped to identify pupils and coloured stripes featured on ties, blazers and hat bands.

After the First World War, girls' clothing continued to grow simpler, more streamlined, short hemlines now set well above the knee. Knitted sweaters or jersey tops and skirts were very fashionable, short-sleeved or sleeveless shift-style dresses in plain or bold geometric-patterned cotton material popular for summer. As spending time outdoors in the sunshine became more common, children increasingly wore short socks with bar shoes, or bare legs and sandals, young heads protected by cotton sun hats. Young girls' hair might be worn long or shoulder-length with a large hair bow, or bobbed with a straight-cut fringe. Older girls wore slightly longer, more ladylike hemlines, with the neutral or flesh-coloured stockings then coming into vogue.

Short, simple shift-like dresses remained popular summer wear between the wars, alongside a new 1930s' fashion for young girls – ornate, party-style dresses fashioned from floral printed fabrics, featuring frills, puffed sleeves and dainty collars. Short hair remained popular for all ages, longer hair often styled in plaits. Following adult modes, dresses grew more shaped in the late 1930s and 1940s, usually made with waist seam and short sleeves, sometimes a gathered, smocked yoke. Separates were also popular, a blouse with knee-length A-line or pleated skirt, and tailored blazer-style jacket or knitted cardigan. Knitwear was very popular, garments including

Snapshot photograph, dated August 1937.

cardigans, jerseys, hats, scarves and gloves. Still, older girls wore longer hemlines, but during the 1930s and 1940s often favoured ankle socks until ready for adult stockings. Jackets and coats remained smart and tailored, with beret, felt or straw hats for formal wear, but few new clothes were acquired during the war and its aftermath.

(iii) Boys

Theoretically, boys were also dressed in different forms of garment according to their size and age. Throughout the 1800s and early 1900s a son's 'breeching' was a recognised event – the point at which he left behind androgynous infants' frocks and was put into his first pair of bifurcated male garments. The age at which this rite of passage occurred ranged from about 3 to 7 years old, depending on the child, each family's circumstances, and the time period: by the late 1800s a common 'breeching' age within the average family was 3½ to 4 years. Later, when aged at least 9–11 years old, or upon reaching a certain height, a boy then advanced from wearing juvenile drawers, knickerbockers or short trousers ('shorts') into more adult trousers or 'longs'. Again, this custom varied with fashion at different dates, individual families' preferences and school regulations.

In 1800 small boys, once 'breeched' were usually put into the so-called 'skeleton suit' – a one-piece trouser outfit, popular since the 1780s. This costume featured a back flap opening, slightly raised waistline obscured by a broad sash, buttons on the bodice/jacket section, the wide frilled white blouse collar featuring at the neck. During the early 1800s, the bodice was increasingly fashioned from dark-coloured wool, the trousers in pale cotton or linen material, their contrasting effect resembling the female chemise gown and coloured spencer jacket. Older boys wore open-necked shirts with more 'grown-up' pantaloons, trousers or breeches, a fashionable waistcoat and tailcoat. Young males of all ages wore longish waved hair – an enduring concession to childhood.

Illustration from *Elliott's Tales for Boys*, 1820s.

During the late 1810s and 1820s, the young boy's skeleton suit assumed a very slender, high-waisted style, the bodice ornamented with buttons and developing a high ruff-like collar, reflecting historicism in women's dress. Soft pump-like shoes replaced Georgian buckled shoes and hair was cut short. By the later 1820s, the skeleton suit was outmoded and a fuller 'tunic suit' was favoured for little boys – a picturesque costume comprising low-necked tunic or dress with short sleeves and open knee-length skirts layered over matching drawers or loose trousers. Often ornamented in the 'hussar' style, with horizontal sets of braid, knots and buttons across the bodice, the ensemble – like girls' outfits – was adapted for outdoor wear with a cape and separate sleeves. Older boys tended to wear a short jacket, double-breasted waistcoat and fitted trousers – the new form of adult male legwear.

In the early-Victorian era, young boys' dress continued to resemble that of their mothers, rather than their fathers' attire. For the newly breeched, a pelisse dress of stout cotton or linen material was fashionable, featuring fitted bodice, narrow waist and full skirt, revealing long cambric drawers beneath. Knee-length dresses and drawers remained usual throughout the mid-1800s, when fashionable taste favoured tartan and plain bold colours ornamented with contrasting braid. Slightly older boys progressed to shorter, thigh- or hip-length tunics belted at the waist, teamed with loose, ankle-length trousers. As before, older sons wore a long-sleeved shirt, long trousers and short, fitted jacket. Hats were always worn outdoors, little boys often decked out in picturesque wide-brimmed headwear. Caps also came into vogue for boys during the 1840s and 1850s, notably the military-style peaked 'kepi' cap.

During the early 1860s, knickerbockers were introduced – knee-length masculine garments that would dominate boys' fashion for at least the next fifty years. Initially cut full in the leg, knickerbockers were gathered or fastened below the knee, securing the long stockings then worn with leather boots. Teamed with a matching waistcoat and jacket, and tailored in woollen cloth, this was a juvenile version of the new adult male three-piece lounge suit. The 1860s' boys' jacket was short with rounded front edges and fastened only at the top, bolero-style. The open jacket and vaguely 'Turkish' shape of the knickerbockers prompted the contemporary term 'zouave' ensemble, referencing the picturesque bolero jackets of the celebrated Algerian Zouave troops who supported the French in the Crimean War. This style of knickerbockers suit persisted throughout the decade, coloured or striped stockings popular for small boys superseded by plainer dark stockings for school.

Following wider fashion trends, during the 1870s and 1880s boys' garments attained a narrower line. The generously cut zouave-style costume was replaced by trimmer jackets, while the knickerbockers slimmed down, often open-ended below the knees. Silk, velvet and plush (cotton velvet) fabrics were favoured for young boys' 'Sunday best' suits and various fanciful styles developed. Quasi-

Fashion plate detail from *Le Petit Courier des Dames*, 1841

Highland dress was admired, as were picturesque velvet costumes with lace collars, following the publication of *Little Lord Fauntleroy* in the mid-1880s. An iconic Victorian children's costume was the sailor suit, based on the naval uniform first introduced for sailors in the 1840s. The young Prince of Wales was portrayed wearing a white cotton drill summer naval uniform in 1846, encouraging a new fashion that slowly spread throughout society. By the early 1880s, versions of the sailor suit were widely fashionable for boys (and girls); also called the 'Jack Tar' suit, this ranged from authentic miniature naval uniform, complete with sailor's cap and lanyard, to simple blue blouson with wide sailor-style collar.

Cdv photograph, dated 1865.

By the late-nineteenth century clothing options were myriad. Knickerbockers and trousers versions of the sailor suit remained popular for leisure wear, available in different materials for all seasons, although a more uniform look was evolving for regular day and school wear. Gathered or open-ended knickerbockers remained usual for young boys – sometimes referred to as 'demi-suits', while older boys from about 9 years and upwards were put into long

Advertisement for boys' clothes from Samuel Brothers tailors, dated 1883.

trousers. Various jacket styles were fashionable, teamed with white shirt and starched white Eton collar for school-age boys. A common choice was a fashionable lounge jacket tailored with neat high lapels and accessorised with a miniature bowler hat, until the popular cloth cap became established during the 1890s. Another favourite was the distinctive Norfolk jacket featuring vertical pleats and a cloth belt: originally an adult sporting style, the Norfolk suit extended to boys by 1880, gaining popularity and still widely worn in 1900.

Late-Victorian styles continued into the Edwardian era, the cloth knickerbockers suit with choice of jackets and neckwear a firm favourite for daywear, until a boy was ready for long trousers. Black woollen stockings, leather boots and a cloth cap completed the outfit. During the early 1900s, younger boys often wore a wide frilled white collar, expressing ornate Edwardian taste, the juvenile sailor suit also popular at this time. Dress in general underwent considerable modifications during the 1910s, growing less cluttered, more natural in style and feel. Small boys were often put into simpler, lightweight outfits comprising blouse-like tunic tops with above-the-knee shorts – socks and shoes largely replacing thick stockings and boots. A growing emphasis on practical play clothes also encouraged stretchy knitted jersey garments during this

School photograph, 1900–01.

decade, although hand-knitted jerseys had long been worn by poorer children. From the 1910s boys throughout society began to adopt soft jersey and shorts sets, while for older schoolboys a more uniform look included caps and blazers in school colours.

After the First World War, the hand-knitted or shop-bought, machine-knitted jersey with integral collar became a mainstay of young boys' wardrobes: worn throughout the 1920s–40s and beyond, for general play and for Elementary school (where regulation uniform was not always required), often the jersey incorporated a knitted tie. Some formal or class-conscious families dressed their young sons in fanciful velvet suits with frilled collars for 'Sunday best', well into the 1920s; similarly, despite the modern trend for short hair, many little boys had longish curly hair.

For older boys, school uniform was well established by the 1920s. Comprising grey flannel shorts, white or grey shirt, knotted tie, jacket or blazer and cloth cap or rounded school cap, this standardised image persisted until the later twentieth century. Moreover, many elements of school uniform and everyday clothing were interchangeable, so weekend wear often included the same formal collared shirt, grey shorts and tailored jacket/blazer that were routinely worn to school. During the

Snapshot photograph, early 1920s.

1930s relaxed, sporty short-sleeved shirts in new breathable fabrics like Aertex were introduced for casual wear and knitted garments were popular; sweaters and slip-overs of plain, cable or Fair Isle knit. A boy's outfit was completed with grey socks and laced leather shoes or sandals, or, for play, the white canvas plimsolls or sneakers used for school PE lessons. Until after the Second World War, outdoor winter-wear comprised a tailored buttoned coat, woollen muffler, knitted hat or cloth cap.

North London school photograph, 1931/1932.

Chapter 2

Following Fashion

Family historians frequently wonder how closely their poorer or working-class ancestors would have been able to follow fashion, as outlined in Chapter 1 – a valid question, to which there is no one single answer. The exact dress worn by any individual depended on many factors including social position, income, geographical location, occupation and personal preferences – and, importantly, the era. Here we examine a number of variables: survival of traditional styles early in our period; increasing spread and impact of metropolitan fashion; escalation of fashion news and clothing technology, bringing affordable fashion to the masses; the effect of photography on shaping visual perceptions and encouraging self-awareness; the impact of advancing age on some of our predecessors' clothing choices; and the popularisation and democratisation of twentieth-century fashion.

Metropolitan Novelties

History has shown how society always absorbs urban culture; usually it is city-living and new metropolitan trends that others aspire to, attempt to emulate and eventually embrace, albeit in modified form. In the early-nineteenth century, high society kept abreast of the latest modes from France – the capital of European fashion – by visiting Paris, or (especially during the Napoleonic Wars, 1803–1815, when the Continent was closed to Britons), by going to London, elegant spa and seaside resorts, or through the verbal and written descriptions of friends or relatives. The influence of innovative urban style on provincial taste at this time characterises the novels and private correspondence of Regency author Jane Austen. For instance, in *Pride and Prejudice* (1813), when Mrs Gardiner from London arrived at the Bennets' Hertfordshire home, her first tasks were to 'distribute her presents and describe the newest fashions'. Jane and her personal associates also reported back on their observations when visiting the city, Jane writing from London in

September 1814: 'I am amused by the present style of female dress; – the coloured petticoats with braces over the white Spencers & enormous Bonnets upon the full stretch, are quite entertaining. It seems to me a more marked *change* than one has lately seen.'

While comfortably placed, socially mobile late-Georgian and Regency ancestors would have had ready access to modern urban amenities; for our working forebears in the provinces and, especially in remoter areas, communications were then relatively slow. The establishment of railway networks from the 1840s onwards revolutionised connections between town and country, gradually bringing disparate locations closer together. However, in the early 1800s, given the poor state of many rural roads, most ordinary people did not regularly travel long distances (unless by local canal or sea transport). For many country dwellers, trips to

Fashion plate from *Ackermann's Repository of Arts*, August 1814

the local market town, seasonal fairs, visits from pedlars and touring salesmen, and interaction with local drapers and garment-makers were the chief means of acquiring new dress ideas. There would have been a fashion time lag of at least a few years in certain contexts and for the early part of our period in particular, it is perhaps more pertinent to consider how local traditions in some regions *differed* from metropolitan dress.

Regional Variations

Dress holds up a mirror, reflecting the world we inhabit, and studying regional clothing customs can often illuminate past lives. England does not boast a legacy of distinct 'folk' costumes representing different geographical regions (as does much of mainland Europe), but in the early to mid-1800s there existed residual local styles carried over from earlier eras, and certain place-related customs. Chapter 3 examines established rural dress items like smocks and red cloaks, and trends such as new factory wear in northern districts. Additionally, seafaring communities also developed their own dress forms, most notably the hand-knitted blue or grey fisherman's 'knit-frock' – the jersey or 'gansey' (dialect term); originating in the Channel Islands in the later 1700s, these were widely worn in coastal – and some inland river – regions throughout the 1800s and early to mid-1900s. At a more local level, fisherwomen from Newhaven in Scotland were known for their brightly striped calf-length petticoats (skirts) in the 1700s and early to mid-1800s; these eventually became a form of 'fossilised' or 'archaic' regional dress, donned for tourists and modelled in popular souvenir photographs.

Ancestors living in Scotland, Wales, Ireland and remoter English districts would undoubtedly have been familiar with local dress traditions in the early 1800s, although contemporary images are scarce and no single in-depth historical survey of the subject exists. Readily accessible evidence indicates that, while principal garments such as ladies' gowns might follow the prevailing fashionable line, small dress accessories like headwear and home-produced items were especially subject to regional variations. For instance, Welsh women were known for their square, fringed woollen shawls and larger mantles called 'whittles', country women from Somerset, Devon and Cornwall also wore whittles or 'West Country rockets', a regional term. Local manufactures and handicrafts frequently shaped aspects of dress in some areas: for example, the remote island of Fair Isle between Orkney and Shetland was – and remains – famed for its production of colourful knitwear in prescribed designs. In Chapter 10 we examine more of the regional dress-related industries in which ancestors worked and that influenced their personal experience of fashion and clothing.

Cdv photograph of Newhaven Fishwife, c.1874–77.

In the late-Georgian and early-Victorian periods, rather than wearing fashionable feminine millinery, females often adopted versions of men's black beaver or felt hats when outdoors: these feature in some of the pioneering regional artistic studies produced in the early-nineteenth century, such as George Walker's *Costume of Yorkshire* (1814). Perhaps the best-known example is the Welsh woman's iconic drum-shaped or tapered black hat resembling men's tall headwear; this mode probably evolved in the 1830s and continued only for thirty to forty years, in certain districts, yet today these hats, worn with colourful flannel petticoats, shawls and aprons, are known the world over as 'Welsh' dress (see coloured image No.10). Indeed we do recognise the 'national' dress of Wales and Scotland, costumes separate from mainstream fashion, comprising traditional local items that subsequently became 'fossilised' – perpetuated in visual imagery and in the popular imagination. Interestingly, it is also in Wales that some of the last examples of recognisable regional working attire were worn; in the 1930s, on the Gower peninsular at cockle and mussel harvesting times, local women still galloped on donkeys out to the beds at low tide, wearing shawls around their heads, short skirts, footless black stockings and rubber-soled shoes.

Technological Advances

Traditional and regional clothing styles are both fascinating and relevant to how earlier generations lived, yet ultimately the story of nineteenth-century dress was one of increasing standardisation, the extension of mainstream metropolitan fashion into many corners of Britain. As industry forged ahead, advancing technology, faster communications, manufacturing progress and rising production were all factors that accelerated the pace of fashion, hastening its dissemination throughout much of society.

From the mid-1800s onwards, improved printing processes, coupled with a soaring population and growing consumer demand, fuelled the proliferation of women's magazines and domestic handbooks. New periodicals and volumes like the *Englishwoman's Domestic Magazine*, launched in 1852, later collected and published as *Mrs Beeton's Book of Household Management* (1861), and *The Queen* (established in 1861) were aimed largely at the expanding middle classes who comprised a significant proportion of mid-Victorian society. With public literacy also on the rise, it was becoming easier for more people to read about – and to view pictures of – the new season's fashions. Many other publications also launched in the mid- to late-Victorian age and by the 1880s even the regular daily and weekly press featured fashion-led articles. Moreover, popular newspapers, journals and magazines became highly illustrated in the later 1800s, bringing a striking new visual element to publishing. By the 1890s, images accompanied many editorial articles and advertisements; photographs and lithographs of clothes, accessories and hair products now became a familiar feature of the printed page.

Publicity in general escalated from the mid-nineteenth century onwards, with dedicated product branding and bold commercial advertising on posters and billboards making it difficult for anyone walking along the street, ascending an omnibus or entering a railway station to remain unaware of the avalanche of Victorian consumer goods. The Industrial Revolution had begun with textile production and now many dress-related items, once hand-made, were being mass-produced in machine-driven factories, from cotton, woollen, linen, silk and mixed-yarn textiles, to ready-made clothes. By 1860, Britain, approaching the height of its prosperity and confidence, was the world leader in industry and many citizens enjoyed vastly increased consumer choice. The economies

Advertisement from Allen Foster & Co. manufacturers, c.1895–96.

of large-scale factory production was also reflected in reduced costs, bringing ever more desirable goods on to the market at keener prices. These developments would have huge implications for the spread of fashion and the dress of ordinary working people.

As early as 1808, Heathcote's invention of a bobbin net machine had introduced a much cheaper alternative to traditional hand-made lace, enabling many women on tight budgets to incorporate the luxury effect of delicate lace into their dress at a fraction of the price. During the 1830s, the importation of the Jacquard loom into Britain radically advanced the production of woven silks, formerly top-end materials way beyond the means of the majority of the population. In the 1840s, John Wright of Birmingham refined existing metal electro-plating processes, the first economical gold- and silver-plated costume jewellery becoming available in the late 1850s. Later, in Chapter 8, we examine how the development of mechanical sewing machines aided the home dressmaker; mechanised sewing, and, from 1860, the cutting out of multiple pieces simultaneously, using the new band-knife, revolutionised the making of garments and footwear in factories and workshops.

New technology throughout the course of the century continued to extend manufacturing possibilities, and this impacted enormously on the way in which most of our ancestors dressed. Ready-made ('off-the-peg') male garments were available at an early date; by the mid-1800s ordinary working men could acquire a smart work or 'Sunday best' suit comprising coat or jacket, waistcoat and trousers in modern styles, at affordable prices. Victorian women's gowns, generally of more complex construction than men's garments, were usually wholly or partly made-to-measure until at least the late 1800s, but before the turn of the century enterprising manufacturers were offering high-fashion, well-priced costumes in a range of materials through mail order, upon receipt of customers' measurements. Otherwise local tailors, dressmakers and milliners advised, as they had always done, on the latest styles; seasonal fashion plates adorned their shop windows and many stocked a wide range of materials.

A significant feature of late-Victorian fashion was the development of many cheap fabrics emulating, for instance, silk velvet (cotton velvet or 'plush') and silk satin (sateen). Along with affordable ready-made items such as ladies' cloaks and capes, stockings, hats and gloves, and men's shirts, hose, hats and neckties, it was possible for many of our wage-earning ancestors to appear, if not richly dressed, then fashionably attired in up-to-date styles. Fashion was becoming more uniform and more widespread, even, apparently, in country areas. In *Lark Rise to Candleford* (1945) Flora Thompson, recalling her early life in rural Oxfordshire during the 1880s and early 1890s, quoted a popular local saying: 'Better be out of the world than be out of the fashion'. In her real-life hamlet of Juniper Hill (fictional 'Lark Rise'), fashion was only 'a year or two behind outside standards'.

Presenting an Image

Besides introducing many more economical fabrics, clothes, accessories and jewellery to a wider public, Victorian technology made an impact in other ways. Recently, social and cultural historians have identified the mid-nineteenth century as a period when glass rapidly became a public phenomenon, precipitated by the abolition of excise tax on glass in 1845. Massive price reductions over the next twenty years prompted significant developments, such the installation of vast plate glass windows in many urban shops and department stores, and the introduction of long 'cheval' mirrors into private homes. Perhaps for the first time, many of our predecessors could now effectively view their own full-length reflections.

Additionally there was the new 'invention' of photography, trialled over many years, refined and announced to the world in 1839. The first commercial *daguerreotype* portrait rooms opened in major cities during the 1840s, followed by more studios offering cheaper ambrotype photographs throughout the 1850s. Portrait photography reached a wide population during the 1860s with the first mass-produced photographic print, the *carte de visite*. Thousands of portrait photographers now operated nationwide from fixed high street premises, or toured country areas as itinerant practitioners. Initially charging significant sums, their fees lowered drastically with increased competition, bringing the occasional photograph within the range of not only the privileged classes, but many working people. By the mid-1860s, people from all walks of life, from royalty and aristocracy to straw plaiters, teachers, farm labourers and post boys could now sit for a formal photograph, their image circulated and surviving for posterity.

The 'cartomania' of the 1860s – or craze for commissioning, exchanging and collecting *carte de visite* portraits – led to the production of the first purpose-designed photograph albums. Initially compiling such albums and displaying their contents was a middle-class pastime, later advancing during the late-nineteenth century. Yet from the outset the new vogue for viewing and discussing photographs of relatives and friends, as well as mass-produced, popular images of the rich and famous – early 'celebrity' photographs – instigated a shift in visual awareness for our Victorian forebears. Mechanical photographs were considered the first truthful images recording authentic human details (albeit sometimes enhanced), and this altered perceptions of the self and of other people. Glorious photographs of members of the royal family, actresses, foreign dignitaries and other key figures exhibited in printers', stationers' and photographers' shop windows demonstrated to a captivated

Cdv photograph, early 1890s.

audience exactly what fashion leaders looked like at a given time; within ordinary families and neighbourhoods, the act of commissioning a photograph and viewing the resulting image must have heightened self-awareness, encouraging a more rigorous self-appraisal than many had experienced before.

Arranging to sit for a portrait photograph was a pre-meditated action, usually pre-booked and often timed to coincide with an important event such as engagement, marriage, birthday or mourning. Invariably it involved wearing 'Sunday best' clothes, or attire appropriate to the occasion – a recognised opportunity for sartorial display. For Victorian women in particular, who typically led a more sheltered, less public role than most men, photography offered an unprecedented chance to present themselves to an audience, perhaps project a sense of the person they wanted to be. Clothing and hairstyles played a major role in the photographic process, to the extent that sometimes visitors to the studio changed their outfit in between exposures. It is also interesting to note that in most family collections of formal Victorian and Edwardian studio photographs, there are typically many more female portraits than those of men – perhaps suggesting that portrait photography was especially important to women's experience of fashion and ideas of self-presentation.

The Generation Gap

People of all ages were photographed between 1850 and 1950, individually, in couples and in larger groups, yet among professional studio photographs of single subjects, images of young adults predominate. Many are aged between their 'teens' (a term not used until the twentieth century) and late 20s: moreover, in some collections multiple different photographs of the same person occur in quick succession, around that stage of life. Evidently in the past, like today, once adolescents and young adults were working and buying their own clothes, many developed a strong interest in fashion, enjoyed the creative possibilities of trialling new styles, and were keen to be pictured modelling their favourite attire. Undoubtedly there were also economic reasons for this pronounced tendency, observed across many private photograph collections. Academic studies of household expenditure show how, long before the advent of photography, young wage-earning people could usually provide adequately for themselves, yet once married, when children came along, one after another, financial outlay escalated and domestic budgets quickly became stretched. In most families, not only would there not have been the funds for portraits of any description, but even provision of decent clothing for everyone became a major challenge.

This traditional economic pattern, experienced down the generations, combined with a lower average life expectancy than today, partly explains the dearth of studio photographs of the middle-aged and elderly, compared with many surviving images of fashionably dressed younger ancestors. It also seems likely that older family members became less enthusiastic about posing for a formal photograph as they aged, especially before the 1900s when home photography and relaxed amateur snapshots became more commonplace. Victorian and Edwardian ancestors generally felt – and were considered to be – 'older' at a much younger stage of life than today, typically experiencing a growing sense of maturity from their late 20s onwards. Personal appearance would generally be toned down, dress and hairstyles growing more conservative or formal, as the older generation distanced themselves from light youthful styles and extreme fashions. Who knows, perhaps some elderly forebears simply did not wish their ageing appearance to be preserved in images destined to survive beyond their lifetime.

In the past, there was a pronounced sense of how members of different age groups should dress. Even in the mid-twentieth century older men retained more facial hair, wearing traditional tailored three-piece suits and outmoded watch chains for longer than the young generation. Throughout the 1800s and early 1900s, by middle age many women had developed an entire wardrobe based on black clothes; sometimes they were widowed and remained in quasi-mourning. More commonly, black was considered a 'safe', sedate choice; it could be worn anywhere, including to church on Sundays and for funerals. The clothes of mature adults were often styled to resemble mainstream dress with a deliberate slight time lag; sometimes more modest garment forms were favoured, especially when high fashion decreed extreme effects, in some cases clothes were worn less frequently, but lasted

Snapshot photograph, dated May 1919.

longer, naturally growing outdated. Particular themes also recur; for instance, elderly Victorian and Edwardian ladies preferred traditional bonnets to fashionable wide-brimmed hats, also choosing capes or cloaks over modish jackets and coats. Perhaps most extraordinary to modern eyes were the ornate white lace caps or widows' headdresses and floor-length black clothes still worn by elderly matrons in the 1920s, when younger women wore simple, colourful garments and short hemlines.

Fashion and Popular Culture

Historically, high fashion followed long-established traditions concerning superior quality, the correct dress for the various classes and for different occasions. However, during the early-twentieth century new, more democratic modes evolved, inspired by modern cultural trends. The growth of active sports in the early 1900s was a decisive factor; sporting dress, in needing to be comfortable, has always pushed forward sartorial boundaries – more on this in Chapter 6. The rise of popular cinema, especially from the 1910s onwards, along with modern forms of music and daring dance moves from America encouraged freer, more youthful styles of dress, including bold evening modes, as described in Chapter 7. New fashion role models also emerged, from glamorous matinée idols and movie gangsters to jazz entertainers, further undermining convention, by popularising unorthodox haircuts, use of cosmetics, and innovative clothing fabrics and styles suitable for dance floors, cocktail bars and jazz clubs.

Sadly some of our poorer ancestors endured extreme poverty in between the two world wars, but many ordinary working people, particularly in southern England, were enjoying a higher standard of living, with access to many affordable consumer goods. Advances in mass-production, including improved

Studio photograph, mid-1930s.

garment sizing systems – essential if clothes were to be bought off-the-peg – furthered the ready-made clothing industry in Britain. Multiple stores such as Woolworths, the Co-op, British Home Stores, C&A and Marks & Spencer proliferated in the high street, selling cheap to moderately priced clothes. Affordable, easy-care synthetic fabrics, most notably the silk substitute rayon, became firmly established in the working- and lower-middle class wardrobe, enhancing the convenience of dress. Older, affluent, conservative or more discerning individuals still patronised their favourite tailor or 'little dressmaker' up until 1950 and beyond, but for the masses, fashion was becoming more ephemeral, economical and fun. Younger people and the upwardly mobile classes aimed for a choice of stylish outfits: they could often follow the latest trends, far less restricted by traditional values, personal income and geographical location than their predecessors.

Chapter 3

Work Wear: Town and Country

For much of the period covered by this book, many ordinary wardrobes were dominated by clothes suitable for work – plain, functional garments worn, usually, from Monday to Saturday, only Sundays and holidays offering a break from the monotony of occupational dress. We begin this theme with rural styles, for in 1800, country dwellers and land workers formed the bulk of the nation's population. However, this was set to change; by the 1851 census, over half lived in towns (albeit including rural administrative centres like Lewes in Sussex and Aylesbury in Buckinghamshire). By 1901, the census recorded around 80 per cent of the population as 'urban', reflecting continuing migration away from the countryside into more densely populated hubs. These shifting occupational patterns and living conditions had profound effects on work wear: traditional late-Georgian agricultural clothing became increasingly urbanised during the nineteenth century.

Rural Styles

(i) Breeches and smocks
In 1800 most men wore knee breeches or pantaloons. For outdoor work, breeches were fashioned from stout cloth or, more commonly, durable buckskin leather, often undone at the knee for easy movement. Generally agricultural labourers' breeches were teamed with laced or strapped leather gaiters or 'leggings' to protect the lower leg, footwear ranging from sturdy leather shoes reinforced with iron nail-studded soles, to short boots. At this early date, men also wore wooden-soled leather clogs in northern counties such as Lancashire and Cumberland. The shirt was a loose garment of linen or cotton, the sleeves rolled up for heavy tasks and when temperatures soared. Many country men possessed only the one set of basic work clothes, a better outfit kept for Sundays and holidays.

A general shortage of clothes among poorer working men partly explains the adoption of a practical 'smock-frock' as an outer layer over the breeches and shirt. The rural smock, widely worn in the later 1700s and 1800s, afforded some protection from the elements, helped to prevent the clothes beneath from becoming soiled, and also concealed dirty or ragged garments that didn't quite meet standards of respectability. Almost exclusively a male item, the smock-frock was worn by both farmers and labourers, chiefly in the rural midlands and southern counties of England. It was uncommon in the north and in coastal regions where fishing predominated and men favoured the comfortable 'knit-frock' (knitted 'gansey' or sweater).

The smock-frock was a loose, long-sleeved knee- or calf-length garment that slipped on over the head or fastened in front. Typically using several yards of fabric, as Rachel Worth explains in *Clothing and Landscape in Victorian England*, early forms were often made from fine bleached linen ('Russia duck'), later more commonly from cotton or drabbet (a coarser twilled cotton or mixed cotton/linen cloth). Smocks also featured 'smocking' – a distinctive embroidery technique used to gather fabric and give 'stretch' in the days before elastic, affording the wearer comfort and greater movement. Modest forms of the embroidery were developing by 1800, although early smocks were relatively plain, compared with the smocking on later garments. More decorative embroidery was becoming characteristic by the 1830s, reflecting the growing elaboration of mainstream fashion. Pioneering historian of rural dress, Anne Buck, established that the most ornate stitching, from hearts, diamonds and spirals, to waves, leaves and floral motifs was applied to smocks made and worn between the 1830s and 1870s.

Many of the smock-frocks worn by our farming ancestors were light-coloured, appearing white/cream, beige, stone or buff, others being brown, olive green or blue. Some experts suggest that these variants were firmly linked to location, and evidently some colours predominated in certain areas; for instance, Worthing Museum and Art Gallery in West Sussex has several brown smocks in the collection, while Newark, famous for its production of blue smocks, popularised these in Nottinghamshire, Lincolnshire and neighbouring counties. However, smocks of a particular colour cannot be pinned down precisely to within a limited geographical area; for instance, blue smocks were also popular in parts of Sussex. Recent research focuses more on their impressive variety throughout the country, wherever these iconic items were worn.

The use of voluminous, protective smocks by country dwellers varied with the job and occasion; their loose folds being potentially

Anonymous print depicting Dorset agricultural workers, c.1840.

dangerous, they were not suitable for certain tasks, especially using threshing machines and other mechanised equipment. Smock-frocks were particularly favoured by shepherds, cowmen, drovers, carters and waggoners, who worked outdoors in all weathers; indeed, heavy-duty smocks might be fashioned with protective shoulder capes and some were given a water-resistant coating of linseed oil. Smock-frocks were also adopted by various other land workers, from millers, through gardeners and seedsmen to ferreters, while rural craftsmen travelled into town to sell their wares, wearing a fresh smock. The most finely embellished smocks surviving in museums today were probably special wedding and 'Sunday best' garments, but functional, workaday smock-frocks were a familiar sight throughout the early to mid-1800s and beyond.

As outlined in Chapter 1, during the 1810s long 'trowsers' entered mainstream fashion and from the 1820s onwards modern trousers began to substitute for traditional breeches in rural areas. The shift to trousers was by no means uniform throughout the country, or among all men; knee breeches persisted for many years, especially among older and poorer labourers, conservative farmers and particularly in outlying districts. Yet, the forward trend was towards modernity, urban styles particularly appealing to the younger generation, and by the 1840s trousers were a familiar item of country dress.

Like breeches, trousers could be made of buckskin, although durable fustian (a robust mixed linen/cotton textile), moleskin (thick cotton fabric with a soft pile) and corduroy (sturdy cotton cloth with a ridged surface) were all strong, functional materials well-suited to working garments. Gaiters for the lower legs were less common with trousers, but remained in use, along with leggings – similar to gaiters and sometimes made of hide. Another custom was to hitch up the trousers up below the knee with a buckled strap, length of string, bootlace or straw, to free the knees, raise hems out of the mud and, allegedly, to prevent field mice running up the trouser legs. These makeshift ties were variously called *yorks*, *bowy-yanks*, *lijahs*, *pitseas* and *whirlers* in different regions – terms deriving from local dialect words for 'leggings' or 'gaiters'.

Traditional smock-frocks were sometimes worn with trousers, but from around the mid-1800s smocks began to decline in favour of regular metropolitan-style clothing. More agricultural labourers were now employed on short-term contracts, often living away from the farms where they worked; being more mobile, they were increasingly receptive to outside ideas and modernising influences. Additionally, mechanised production of men's clothes occurred early and affordable mass-produced modern suits were available in most parts of Britain by the 1840s/50s. Consequently, the mid- to late-Victorian farm labourer's upper garments typically comprised a jacket or jerkin and waistcoat, worn over a collarless shirt, the jacket removed for strenuous tasks, a bright red handkerchief often tied around the neck. Jackets and waistcoats could be made of flannel (a soft woollen fabric), but, like trousers, generally from thick, hard-wearing cotton or cotton/linen mix materials including corduroy, fustian and moleskin. For summer, an unbleached drill (stout cotton) or lightweight canvas jacket was popular by the late 1800s, a casual, ready-made garment broadly termed a 'slop', regional names including the northern 'kitle' and Oxfordshire 'sloppy'.

Conventional smock-frocks continued to be worn chiefly by older men in the later 1800s, especially for 'Sunday best', as evidenced by late-Victorian studio photographs. But in many districts by the 1870s and 1880s the average farm worker's attire was looking increasingly like an urban suit. The novelist and poet Thomas Hardy documented the 'rage' for fashionable 'pilot coats' or 'pilots' among younger men – dark, short jackets, often double-breasted, and popularly worn with black trousers. As noted by Rachel Worth in *Clothing and Landscape in Victorian England*, Hardy, who rued the disappearance of many rural traditions during his lifetime, reflected in *The Dorsetshire Labourer* (1883) how back in the 1850s and 1860s, the typical crowd at a hiring fair displayed a colour of 'whity brown flecked with white'; workers arrived in smock-frocks and gaiters, the shepherds with their crooks, thatchers with a straw tucked into their hat and so on. Conversely, by the early 1880s the predominant colour was dark, many wearing black town garb or brown tweed suits with little or no outward sign of their particular trade.

Stout leather boots were the usual footwear for late-Victorian farm workers and in wet conditions these were sometimes given a waterproof dressing of candle grease, a lining of hay inside the boot providing extra warmth. Some older labourers cut the feet out of their stockings, preferring a wrapping of dock leaves and linen strips – less liable to cause sores. Felt, animal hair or summer straw hats were traditionally broad-brimmed and, for much of the nineteenth century, the 'billycock' was a firm favourite – a soft felt wide-brimmed 'wide-awake' style. However, from the 1870s country headgear also changed and a stiff bowler-style hat with narrower brim grew fashionable. Still called the 'billycock' by some, this was not the conventional hat by that name but a smarter style to complement urban suits. In the 1890s, a version of the cloth cap formerly worn mainly for sports began to be adopted by workers everywhere and this rapidly became a popular country style.

Traditionally garments were layered for warmth, but in severe wintry conditions a fleecy overcoat was sometimes worn by shepherds, drovers and others working outside. Additionally, certain agricultural crafts and trades required special clothing or accessories: for instance, hedgers, who handled thorny branches, wore thick leather hedging mittens and fashioned coarse sacking smocks or aprons to protect their clothes; reapers used gloves to guard their hands from thistles and hard corn stalks; while thatchers usually wore protective leather knee pads over the trousers and a 'palm' – a leather pad strapped to the palm of the hand – when working with spars and cut reeds.

Postcard photograph of haymaking, Hurstpierpoint, West Sussex, early 1900s.

In the early 1900s, the English countryside continually evolved, yet some of the old ways drifted on. Traditional smock-frocks, sometimes oiled for a waterproof effect, were worn as late as the 1920s by older shepherds in parts of Norfolk, Suffolk and Sussex, but these were rare survivals: most Edwardian land workers wore contemporary metropolitan-style garments in corduroy and other hard-wearing materials. Trousers tied under the knee remained a familiar sight, while modern forms of country knee breeches and knickerbockers developed. Early-twentieth-century breeches were sometimes tailored wide in the thigh with reinforced inner legs, jodhpur-style; becoming popular for equestrian activities (see Chapter 6), breeches or jodhpurs were also teamed with gaiters and high leather boots by drivers of horse-drawn farm vehicles, delivery carts and local transport in rural areas.

Other innovations occurred in farm wear during the first half of the twentieth century. Long rubber wellington boots with waterproof linings were being worn by the 1920s and, although slow to catch on nationwide, eventually ousted the traditional leather-based methods of protecting lower legs and feet. Jackets and waistcoats were discarded when necessary, but removal of the shirt was still considered indecent. During the 1930s, all-in-one dungaree-style bib and brace work overalls were introduced – a practical protective outfit that reduced the need for aprons in any sphere of farm work. Wide-brimmed straw hats might be used in summer, but modern hats generally featured small brims and the working man's cloth cap was now regular headwear in town and country. As in many areas of work, prior to the First World War the farmer, farm manager or overseer often wore a formal bowler hat; considered important for defining occupational rank in the 1800s and early 1900s, this practice eventually declined, along with other time-honoured sartorial customs.

(ii) Bonnets and shawls

In 1800 many country women wore a tubular high-waisted dress that followed the fashionable neo-classical line, typically made from warm wool or flannel in winter, lighter calico (substantial cotton) or linen in summer. Hemlines were generally lifted off the ground when outdoors, otherwise, when working, skirt material was draped up at the sides, *polonaise*-style, or the front edges pinned back, revealing a coloured petticoat (late-Georgian term for skirt). Among labouring women, common alternatives to the one-piece dress were a separate bodice (or 'jacket-bodice') and skirt, or the 'bed-gown' – an informal three-quarter-length wrap-over garment layered over the petticoat/skirt and often worn open below the waist (see coloured image No.1). Both styles were worn with a linen waist-apron and a white or coloured linen kerchief folded over the shoulders, its points tied or tucked in at the front. Heads were covered with a white mob cap (linen day cap) and topped with a felt hat in winter, a straw hat or fashionable narrow straw poke bonnet in summer. Another functional style at this date was a round bonnet with fabric hood gathered on to a cane brim: shielding eyes from the glare and protecting the face from sunburn, this later evolved into the iconic Victorian sun bonnet.

An outdoor lifestyle demanded extra protection in cold weather and style-conscious country women might wear the simple yet fashionable spencer jacket, or longer pelisse coat. However, in many rural areas a popular garment, admired for its warmth and cheerful effect, was a capacious red woollen cloak – the red-hooded cloak immortalised in the folk tale *Little Red Riding Hood*. Sometimes called a 'cardinal', this picturesque yet functional garment was often depicted in early-nineteenth-century paintings, being closely associated with country women in the late-Georgian period. Although worn as ordinary day dress, it was also smart enough for 'Sunday best', and a fine silk-lined example survives in the Gallery of English Costume, Manchester. An alternative to the cloak was a large shawl, and as fashion favoured fuller skirts from the 1830s, a shawl wrapped closely around the upper body proved more convenient. Shawls were extremely versatile, could be worn with a light cotton print dress in summer, or in colder weather a heavier gown of 'stuff' – a warm worsted material. The British shawl industry had flourished since the late 1700s and various types, for instance 'Scotch plaid' shawls, were popular for everyday use.

Traditionally, certain agricultural jobs were performed by women, for example that of dairymaid, an occupation that often involved living-in and included various tasks. Dairying was considered wholesome and appropriate for young single females, who, despite doing some of the most arduous farm work, were popularly portrayed as feminine, rosy-cheeked and wearing picturesque clothes – colourful dresses or bed-gowns, neat kerchiefs and dainty caps. By contrast, in the early/mid-1800s mixed-sex agricultural 'gangs' operated in some regions – groups of men, women and children working together under a male 'gang-master'. These earned a bad reputation for exploitation and for the coarse lifestyle that the system engendered; therefore it may have been female gang members who observers recorded removing outer clothes and working in the fields in neckerchiefs, half-laced stays and shifts, with petticoats pinned between their legs. Either way, in 1867 the 'immoral' activities of gangs were curtailed by the Agricultural Gangs Act, Victorian sensibilities deeming it unsuitable for women to undertake hard labour outdoors alongside men. Naturally, everybody helped with the harvest, especially haymaking, fruit and hop picking; otherwise far fewer outdoor agricultural jobs remained open to females. Married woman were believed to be best employed in domestic tasks and running the home.

With Victorian female farm workers less 'visible' than men, it is harder to pinpoint some of the details of women's country wear. Some historians suggest that variants of the male smock-frock may have been adopted for duties like mucking out animal sheds, but evidence is scant and probably aprons were worn for such chores. Sturdy leather boots were common country footwear, some women, like men, also wearing stout nailed wooden clogs with leather uppers. This was especially true in Derbyshire and counties further north, although clogs were also known in southern districts like Somerset. Additionally, pattens – formerly worn by all classes, in both town and country – were still used by women in rural areas. Having toe-caps, tough wooden soles and hardwearing 'irons', pattens worn over shoes protected regular footwear from dirt and damage in rugged, muddy lanes. Both clogs and pattens finally fell from use in the mid-Victorian period, partly because of their old-fashioned image, but also due to the growing availability, from the 1860s onwards, of ready-made boots and shoes.

As with menswear, women's rural dress increasingly followed mainstream, urban-led fashion and gradually traditional sartorial customs declined. By the mid-1800s the Georgian jacket-bodice and bed-gown were no longer worn in England, although sometimes garments were draped up for work, as before. The usual mid-century style was a fitted gown with waist seam, typically of warm flannel or linsey woolsey (coarse wool/linen or wool/cotton fabric) in winter, or plain, checked or striped cotton material in summer. Few working-class country women favoured the vast, cumbersome crinoline frame of the late 1850s/60s or the full protruding bustle fashionable in the early 1870s and again mid- to late 1880s, although some adopted modest

Cdv photograph of Bedfordshire centenarian wearing outmoded red hooded cloak, 1870s.

versions of these styles. Working dresses were protected by a long work apron, extra-strong aprons fashioned from sacks or sugar bags useful for heavy or dirty work. Regarding outerwear, the red hooded cloak was rarer by mid-century, although some elderly women retained the beloved garment worn throughout their lives. Shawls – high fashion until the 1860s – remained common in country districts, functional masculine-style overcoats like the Ulster, with detachable hood, coming into female use from the 1870s.

Cotton sunbonnets – regarded today as archetypal female country wear and preserved in museums as iconic symbols of England's agricultural past – first evolved in the 1840s and initially resembled fashionable ladies' bonnets and morning caps. However, their shape and construction rapidly evolved, becoming a distinctive rural mode in which the wide, circular face-opening characteristic of fashionable mid-century bonnets was replaced by practical 'curtains' of fabric protecting the wearer's cheeks and back of her neck from sunburn. Made from plain or printed cotton in diverse patterns, from floral motifs to stripes, country sunbonnets also retained their original frills and tucks as ornamental features. Surviving examples are mainly machine-stitched but finished (carefully hemmed and decorated) by hand, or roughly hand-sewn into a simple shape, suggesting that these accessories were either home-made by the wearer, or partly/completely by a local seamstress. Sometimes fine cane or cord was threaded through stitched channels around the outer edge framing the face, producing a firmer shape and keeping fabric in place in windswept fields.

Distinctive cotton sunbonnets remained popular during the 1800s and well into the 1900s in some locations. In *Lark Rise to Candleford* Flora Thompson described the Oxfordshire female field workers of the 1880s/early 1890s:

> They worked in sun bonnets, hob-nailed boots and men's coats, with coarse aprons of sacking enveloping the lower part of their bodies. One … was a pioneer of trousers; she sported a pair of her husband's corduroys; the others compromised with ends of old trouser legs worn as gaiters.

Also ahead of their time were hardy female Fen labourers, who, as early as the 1890s, wore knee-length dresses and high leather boots for weeding in the mud. Another innovation of the decade, following improvements in rubber manufacture, were rubber galoshes, worn in rain and mud to protect regular footwear.

Women took over much essential farm work during the two world wars. The Women's Land Army (WLA) was first formed in 1917 to provide a full-time female work force, with sections covering agriculture, timber cutting and forage. The uniform issued to recruits comprised a belted knee-length overall tunic, breeches (rarely worn by women before the war), working boots, gaiters and a felt hat. In some areas, leggings and clogs were also supplied in the summer of 1917, warm jerseys and mackintoshes from the autumn. Following suit, other women covering for men away at war also adopted breeches or trousers for farm work, or wore calf-length skirts with boots.

A new WLA was created in 1939, the Second World War land girl's official uniform comprising a cream aertex shirt, green woollen jersey, brown cord knee breeches, long socks, brown lace-up shoes and a brown felt hat, a green beret distinguishing those in the Timber Corps section, formed in 1942. Masculine breeches and trousers were now more widely

Advertisement for work wear from Barkers of Kensington, early 1940s.

accepted for women on farms, standard issue work wear for land girls including overall coats, mackintoshes, dungarees, rubber boots, and sou'westers. In practice, land army work clothes varied: a blouse or sweater might be teamed with dungaree-style overalls and headscarf, while in summer trousers were often adapted into shorts. Some land girls who came from poorer backgrounds enjoyed a better wartime wardrobe than they had in civilian life.

Looking back on the history of rural dress and work wear, as worn by generations of our ancestors, we see how, during the nineteenth century, Georgian agricultural modes declined. By the mid-1800s, typical farm clothes were being styled to resemble mainstream, metropolitan dress, albeit often fashioned in sturdier, more practical materials. Some traditional country items continued into the new century, even between the wars, but as the last generation of wearers passed and farming changed, all agricultural clothes were updated. Many artists, writers and social observers mourned the disappearance of picturesque labourers' smocks, cotton sunbonnets, red cloaks and other rustic garments as they fell from use. These iconic items symbolised a vanished way of life, an idealised bucolic landscape of honest labour, authenticity and simple pleasures, in contrast to the hectic, mechanised modern world. Today examples of archaic rural dress surviving in museum collections are sometimes seen as representing a form of English folk costume.

Factory Dress

As technological progress transformed Britain's economy and society during the 1800s, new, better-paid job opportunities in mills, factories and workshops prompted earlier generations to leave their country roots and join the expanding urban labour force, their hours and productivity thereafter regulated by machinery. The transition from traditional rural crafts and cottage industries to large-scale, mechanised factory production did not occur all at once, or nationwide, but at different rates; initially the changes occurred mainly in the north and midlands, where industry and manufacturing relied heavily on the labour of the working classes, especially women and children. In southern areas of England, farming remained important, although eventually, during the twentieth century, economies of scale and mass-production impacted on manufacturing everywhere.

(i) Early mill clothes
The first English factories were textile mills. When Samuel Greg built a cotton mill at Quarry Bank, Styall, Cheshire in 1784, the indentures of some of his young apprentices indicated receipt of clothes, as well as food and training. Some employers also offered clothing prizes to

their workforce to encourage production, like Richard Arkwright at his Derbyshire cotton-spinning mill during the 1780s. Frustratingly, details are imprecise and with visual images scarce for the early industrial age, we may assume that the first factory staff, like other manual workers, wore functional variants of contemporary styles.

By 1800, male mill and factory workers would have dressed in regular breeches with the short jacket favoured by general labourers, including farm workers, bricklayers and navvies. Longer coats were impractical, as were the loose smocks that some may have formerly worn as agricultural workers, their flowing fabric unsuited to mechanical operations. Men could also remove their jackets and inner waistcoats in the workplace, going 'undressed' in lightweight shirt sleeves and breeches, later trousers. By contrast, female clothes were highly inconvenient in hot and humid, or dusty, airless conditions, long skirts easily caught in moving machinery. Hemlines were shortened to clear the floor, but all loose material was dangerous, layers of underwear stifling.

One positive aspect of the Lancashire cotton manufacturing industry was that workers in the region (and increasingly elsewhere), were no longer limited to wearing basic working garments of traditional coarse wool and linen fabric; many new cotton materials were being produced

The doubling room at Dean Mills cotton mill, Lancashire, *Illustrated London News*, 1851.

and much was affordable, also cool, comfortable and easily washed. Of the various different grades becoming available, stouter calicoes were ideal for work clothes, while a particularly useful new fabric was corduroy, a tough thick-ribbed cotton velvet that became popular for labouring men's suits, in town and in country. Although all British textile products were widely marketed and distributed, it seems possible that workers involved in their manufacture may have had early easy access to materials as they came off the loom. It would be interesting to discover, for example, whether mill hands were able to purchase offcuts or seconds at a discount – or ever received cloth from their employer, in lieu of, or alongside wages.

During the early 1800s, a special type of protective apron evolved for factory work – a simple garment first depicted on young girls and boys from local mills in George Walker's *Costume of Yorkshire* (1814). Made of white cotton or linen and drawn on over the head, it resembled a sleeveless bodice front and back, attached to an apron skirt at the front – a garment for covering the ordinary clothes underneath. Considered to constitute the earliest form of pinafore, this new garment was adopted in mills and factories from the late-Georgian era onwards, distinguishing their workforce from home weavers, who generally retained the traditional waist apron. Otherwise, dress – often a powerful indicator of change – was slow to adapt to the special conditions of the new mills and factories.

(ii) Factory dress codes

Broadly, individual employers defined what their workers should wear and evidently this varied between different workplaces. When the vast, circular cage crinoline frame began to be adopted by women throughout society in the late 1850s, some mill owners intervened. In 1860, the management of Samuel Courtauld & Co., in Essex issued a dress code, assuring female staff that, while they approved of 'comely young women' appearing neat and tidy, they felt duty-bound to prohibit items that hindered the wearer's work or that of others, especially,

> The present ugly fashion of HOOPs and CRINOLINE, as it is called, is … quite unfitted for the work of our Factories. Among the power Looms it is almost impossible, and highly dangerous; among the Winding and Drawing Engines it greatly impedes the free passage of Overseers, Wasters &C., and is also inconvenient to all.

> At the Mills it is equally inconvenient, and still more mischievous, by bringing the dress against the Spindles, while it also sometimes becomes shockingly indecent when the young people are standing upon the Sliders.

Many factory and mill girls were urged to leave behind their cumbersome crinolines and, later in the 1870s and 1880s, projecting bustles when they came to work, overseers even being appointed to check for the offending under-structures. Plain, decent frocks with few petticoats were encouraged as sensible factory wear, with a shawl for warmth. Traditional aprons or the new pinafores were also worn, some pinafores being styled with short sleeves to cover more of the clothes beneath. Long hair was potentially dangerous when operating moving machinery and had to be pinned up securely, or worn in a net, hairnets and *cauls* also popular fashion accessories in the 1860s and early 1870s. Iron-studded wooden-soled clogs with leather uppers became the usual footwear in the factories and mills of northern England – economical shoes that were practical and hard-wearing. Contemporary accounts describe how the sound of hundreds of clogs ringing on the cobbles as mill-hands walked to work could be heard for miles around. In practice, many removed their clogs at work, finding bare feet less hazardous on oily floors.

(iii) Protective clothing

For most of the Victorian era, the law did not enforce provision of any protective clothing for mill and factory staff, and even in heavy industry workers were woefully ill-equipped. Rudimentary steps were taken in some quarters; for instance, in the most hazardous jobs heavy-duty steel-toe reinforced leather boots or shoes evolved for foot protection and sometimes these eventually replaced clogs. In certain textile dyeing and printing works, special aprons incorporating protective leg-shields were devised, but in most factories no 'official' modifications were prescribed. Because of the impractical nature of women's fashions, female workers were most at risk; for instance, in 1894 a 14-year-old fractured her leg when her skirt became caught in the driving band of a carding engine in a Lancashire factory.

Wooden clogs, calf-length skirt, thick dark stockings and chequered shawl were the typical wear of female textile mill workers in the early 1900s, hard-wearing clogs still closely associated with northern industries and worn in some regions until the Second World War. Coveralls or overall coats were now the new, modern style of working garments. A surviving blue and white striped cotton overall in Manchester Art Gallery, worn by an employee from the CWS Jam Works, Greater Manchester, c.1900, is long-sleeved and almost ankle-length, amply covering the wearer's clothes, as well as fulfilling new hygiene requirements. Pinafores continued in the cotton factories where they had first evolved, although in 1926 the Woollen and Worsted Textile Regulations made overalls and head coverings compulsory.

(iv) Wartime factory fashions

During the First World War, millions of women entered factory work, taking over jobs vacated by men in the armed services. Following Factory Act guidelines, 'munitionettes' working in hazardous munitions factories were provided with calf-length overalls treated with flame-retardant chemicals, although these were of little use in major industrial accidents like the Silvertown, West Ham, explosion of January 1917. Most munitions factory overalls were khaki, blue sometimes denoting supervisors or forewomen. Caps to contain long tresses were obligatory, many women cutting their hair short for the first time, instigating a new fashion. All metal items that could possibly cause sparks, including hairpins and steel-boned corsets, were strictly prohibited on the factory floor. New face creams claimed to contain 'special oxygen properties' to preserve the softness and purity of complexions exposed to the 'injurious grit and grime' of the munitions factories; but nothing could prevent the horrific yellowing skin of 'canary girls' working in shell-filling workshops with lethal quantities of TNT. Some female war workers in heavy industry adopted a practical short overall coat or tunic and loose ankle-length trousers. These masculine trousers were donned temporarily, for basic protection and to demonstrate the wearer's role in the factory, mill, shipyard, railway shed or ironworks: duly discarded after the war, none are known to have survived.

During the 1920s and 1930s, tough cotton drill or canvas bib-and-brace overalls (dungarees), and bifurcated boiler suits with large pockets began to be worn in certain industries, replacing traditional aprons and overall coats. Throughout the Second World War, women again operated deafening and dangerous machinery, frequently handling hazardous materials. Clothed in stout, shapeless utilitarian dungarees and boiler-suit overalls, many also used hairnets or headscarves to preserve their hair from polluted factory environments, and as a safety measure. The scarf turban, symbolic of twentieth-century factory work, became a major wartime fashion; simple jersey turbans could be bought, or women fashioned home-made versions, winding a scarf around the head, the ends secured under a forehead knot.

Cosmetics were also widely worn in wartime factories, partly to offset the masculine image created by unfeminine clothes, and again to help protect the complexion from toxic chemicals. British munitions factory workers received a special allowance for face creams in 1942, and periodically a Max Factor sales representative arrived with free beauty products, boosting workers' morale. Wartime factory staff worked long shifts and were usually busy precisely during shop

Postcard photograph of factory workers, c.1915–18.

opening times, but sympathetic employers allowed a free half-day, or two free 'shopping break' hours per week. Essential factory staff were also permitted to register in advance for rationed goods. Previously symbolic of gruelling toil and poverty, factory labour was elevated to a prime position within the wartime economy, work wear receiving a modern makeover.

Business Modes

As the Industrial Revolution transformed Britain's landscape, infrastructure and economy during the 1800s, new occupations evolved and smart, efficient urban attire was needed for a new generation of manufacturers and business managers, financiers, tradesmen, and office personnel.

(i) An urban 'uniform'

In 1800, middle-class gentlemen were likely to be country squires on horseback, but as the modern world became shaped by industry and trade, menswear began to diverge from female modes, growing more standardised and 'masculine'. As outlined in Chapter 1, the key development of the 1820s and 1830s was the establishment of full-length fitted 'trowsers', which rapidly superseded breeches and pantaloons as regular street wear. These functional, restrained garments in turn prompted the adoption of ankle boots (usually concealed by trouser hems) and smart knee-length frock coat, the coat and trousers together creating a more unified and substantial set of clothes. This was the prototype of the modern city suit favoured by industrialists, bankers and men of commerce – the rising middle classes or *bourgeoisie* at the cutting edge of progress.

The early-Victorian urban suit typically comprised frock coat, trousers, waistcoat, shirt, neckwear and high hat. Initially some individuals of artistic, eccentric or flamboyant tendencies, including public figures like Charles Dickens and Benjamin Disraeli, were known for their display of personal taste through patterned waistcoats (traditionally the focus of a man's outfit), bold silk cravats and prominent jewellery. However, as industrial society became more entrenched and working hours increasingly regulated, the growing consensus was that a respectable man should not attract comment through his attire, but cultivate a discreet, businesslike image. During the 1840s and 1850s, slender city frock coats and trousers were crisply tailored from dark cloth, while new forms of overcoat and topcoat, including the *paletot surtout*, the Chesterfield and dependable Ulster, evolved for modern omnibus and rail travel. Sombre, standardised black and grey garments not only masked smut and soot stains from smoke-belching chimneys and steam trains, but, along with tall top hat, businesslike watch chain and starched shirt collar, also exuded an air of seriousness and reliability.

Mid-nineteenth-century literary accounts by Charles Dickens, Friedrich Engels and other writers began to describe the seething thoroughfares of industrial London (and by inference other expanding cities) where extremes of wealth and poverty co-existed and people from all social backgrounds mingled in the street. The growing uniformity of the dark city frock coat, plain trousers and top hat provided a certain anonymity, demonstrating conformity to an accepted ideal. However, beneath this urban 'disguise' it was becoming even more important for a man to demonstrate what kind of person he was – and to be able to accurately 'read' the appearance of others. This applied particularly to the expanding middle classes, keen to prove themselves in the fast-changing workplace and establish their professional and social position. Consequently, even more complex urban dress 'codes' arose around subtle details such as a man's coat buttons or the condition of his starched white shirt collar.

When the male wardrobe began to expand and diversify in the 1850s and 1860s, the role of existing garments changed and shifts occurred in accepted forms of city dress. From the 1870s onwards, the once-ubiquitous frock coat and top hat became progressively outmoded for regular day and work wear. Conversely, the relaxed lounging jacket, initially a semi-casual garment, was now being teamed with matching waistcoat and trousers and increasingly worn as a coordinated 'set of dittos', or everyday

Cdv photograph, early 1860s.

suit, with the modern bowler hat. Between these ultra-formal and relatively casual choices was the stylish morning coat with single- or double-breasted fastening and sloping front edges. A versatile garment much admired by the late 1870s and 1880s, the debonair morning coat, slender in cut, featured small, high lapels, with silk braid binding the collar, cuffs and front edges for a neat finish. Fashionable suiting materials for town included smooth worsteds, cheviot cloths, even black cashmere, the dark coat often teamed with narrow grey pin-striped trousers, known colloquially as 'spongebag trousers'. The image was sleek and elegant, accentuated by the fashionable tall-crowned bowler hat during the later 1880s and 1890s. Fresh starched shirt collars grew higher, while cravats and knotted ties offered a choice of neckwear.

Smart morning suits were favoured in the higher occupations and by many of the office clerks who comprised a significant proportion of the late-Victorian urban workforce. However, among all the middle-class employees broadly termed 'black coat' or 'white collar' workers, there were considerable variations in job status and income, from members of the professions and company directors, down through the ranks to junior clerks, even categories of shopkeeper. Each man had to choose his clothes wisely according to his position, financial means, the season, precise occasion and even the time of day. The 'correct' street or work wear also entailed appropriate accessories, from boots and socks/stockings, through neckwear to gloves, cane/umbrella and hat.

In the 1890s and early 1900s, the stately frock coat and top hat enjoyed a brief revival, presenting a classic image. Typically, it was worn open, revealing fitted waistcoat and gleaming watch chain, set off with a crisp starched winged collar and cravat, bow tie or long knotted tie. A formal, distinguished style favoured by late-Victorian politicians, professionals including doctors, solicitors, bank managers and other senior businessmen, this nonetheless proved the swansong of the frock coat and top hat – a retrograde look henceforth reserved mainly for weddings and society events. It was the suave morning coat, fashioned from plain black or dark grey cloth and worn with grey pin-striped trousers, or the ever more popular three-piece lounge suit that would form the basis of street wear in the twentieth century.

During the Edwardian period, sartorial standards continued much as before. Among the many 'codes' governing city dress were a general dislike of brown clothes and of 'loud' ties, many of the old schools and universities even developing sober versions of their distinctive colourful striped ties, specifically for wear in town. A sparkling white shirt was essential for business wear, growing numbers of 'white collar' workers wearing high standing or winged collars, heavily starched or fashioned from the new material, celluloid. Dedicated shirt launderers and collar finishers developed as prominent trades in town centres and the suburbs, helping ambitious office staff to maintain an impeccable image at work. After the upheavals of the First World War, in a volatile atmosphere of perceived and real job insecurity, most of our male ancestors in work at that time resumed a traditional pre-war formality in their dress. With long-term employment prospects in mind, salaried men took care to follow office protocol, ensuring that their attire reflected their position and career aspirations.

In the late 1920s, men working in the City or central London generally wore a version of what were called 'London clothes'; broadly speaking a dark suit, shoes and overcoat, bowler hat, crook-handled umbrella and gloves. The formal morning suit – black jacket and 'spongebag' striped trousers – was rare beyond the City and the higher professions, although some provincial managers and company directors wore smart morning suits to reinforce their position. Conversely, it was viewed

MEN'S WEAR SECTION

Distinguished Tailoring in Clothes Ready for Wearing

Harrods Ready-to-Wear Clothes have attained such a degree of perfection that many men always choose suits which can be worn right away. They know that whatever their type of figure there will be a size and fitting which will ensure a perfectly made suit at prices which are consistently moderate

SUITS FOR BUSINESS AND FORMAL WEAR

BLACK MORNING COAT

Harrods menswear advertisement, dated 1929.

as presumptuous when ordinary clerks appeared to be dressing above their rank, although contemporaries remarked that when lower-salaried workers adopted more senior modes, there was a noticeable difference in the quality of their clothes. As the economy became more fragile in the 1930s, in conventional office-based jobs it was considered important to maintain high standards and observe clear distinctions between different occupational grades.

Lawyers, doctors, dentists, bankers and company directors were expected to dress carefully and soberly, in line with the seriousness of their work and weight of their responsibility. London conventions set the tone in the south, yet, as Catherine Horwood notes in *Keeping up Appearances: Fashion and Class Between the Wars*, some of the large northern manufacturing towns and cities did not observe 'London' etiquette. There, few businessmen wore sombre morning suits at all by the early 1930s, the favoured mode among industrialists being a modern three-piece pinstripe suit with flamboyant accessories: bold patterned ties and tie-pins, floral buttonholes and silk handkerchiefs.

During and after the Second World War (1939–45), clothes rationing and dull, standard-issue demob suits largely dictated men's street wear as the mid-twentieth century drew near. While in more relaxed office or technical/artisan environments men might substitute the formal tailored waistcoat for a comfortable knitted slip-over or vest, lounge jacket and trousers, shirt and knotted tie continued as 'respectable' city wear, with appropriate hat. In the City of London where dress was most formal, the businessman's pin-striped suit and iconic bowler hat continued into the 1960s.

(ii) Office angels

Businesslike urban street dress developed much later for women, that is, when more of our female ancestors entered the commercial workplace. During the 1870s and 1880s, significant numbers of lower-middle and middle-class females began to gain office-based positions as civil servants; bank, insurance, sales, accounts and general office clerks; telegraphists; telephone operators; and 'typewriters' (later called typists) – a trend that continued in the following decades. Usually, young single women secured this type of employment, joining male colleagues in 'white collar' positions; they generally left work upon marriage, to resume traditional domestic duties.

New kinds of women's work-clothing were now called for – smarter than casual home wear but not too 'done up', to use a contemporary expression. Here sporting dress exerted an influence, since middle- and upper-class women already wore plain, tailored costumes in robust, unostentatious woollen cloth and serge (traditionally associated with uniforms and masculine workwear) for pursuits like yachting and horse-riding (see Chapter 6). During the mid- to late 1870s, royal role model, Princess Alexandra pioneered immaculate suits in serge and in tweed (historically used for men's country sporting wear) and her keynote moulded knitted 'Jersey' costumes. A stylish and much-admired fashion leader, her photographs were widely circulated, helping to popularise chic yet practical jacket-bodice and skirt outfits that provided a blueprint for late-Victorian female urban work wear.

During the 1880s, the vogue for functional tailored gowns or suits grew, being ideal for the new generation of female clerical staff. A formal, efficient appearance was desirable in bank or office, and with time-keeping strict, some women wore a masculine watch and chain, using a special bodice watch pocket. While the elongated *cuirass* line dominated the fashionable silhouette in the early 1880s, a sleek hip-length jacket-bodice in dark cloth and narrow shoe-length skirt were the norm – a severe style that, unadorned, appeared suitably businesslike. From c.1883–84, the close-fitting bodice gained exceedingly narrow sleeves and a high, tight collar, the plain overskirt draped in front while the back formed a bustle projection. This was a more complex, 'upholstered' look, but the use of plain materials and fashion for sombre shades – black, deep brown, maroon and bottle green – were suited to work costumes, accessorised with smart hat, leather gloves and bag or briefcase.

During the 1890s, the 'tailor-made costume' comprising front-fastening jacket with lapels, separate blouse and flared floor-length skirt to match the jacket was widely adopted by many women. While fashionable 'tailor-mades' in attractive colours, worn with lace, embroidered, frilled or flounced blouse and elaborate hat looked sufficiently dressy and feminine for Sundays, holidays and shopping in town, plainer variants were smart and respectable, perfect for work. Tailored from functional woollen and serge materials like those already popular, or in lightweight summer linen, the 'tailor-made' was truly a suit for all seasons, and almost any occasion. Available as a bespoke tailored commission, or partly or wholly 'ready-made', such outfits were also assembled by keen home dressmakers (see Chapter 8).

The no-nonsense tailored costume grew ever more popular in the early 1900s: ideal for work, travel, walking and cycling, it seemed to epitomise the more active, confident female of the time, dubbed the 'New Woman'. Early film footage shows late-Victorian and Edwardian women striding purposefully down the street or swiftly ascending steps, lifting their skirts off the ground with one hand, a bag, book or umbrella in the other. When worn with a plainly styled 'shirtwaist' blouse, starched 'City Day Dress': illustration from *The Family Friend*, 1890.

collar and bow tie or long knotted tie, the female tailored costume closely mirrored the masculine work suit. Appropriate for most office positions and worn as a mass female 'uniform' in the years preceding the First World War, the businesslike white blouse gave rise to the term 'white blouse' revolution.

During and after the war, young middle-class women from quite diverse backgrounds often found clerical, administrative and teaching work although, despite the Sex Disqualification (Removal) Act of 1919, the marriage bar operating in the Civil Service and in schools meant that for many employment ended abruptly upon marriage. More broadly, female office jobs throughout industry soared between 1911 and the 1930s, although few women were managers and apart from (unmarried) teachers, only a few hundred were qualified professionals; many were secretaries, typists and clerks.

In 1922, the *Girls' Favourite* magazine recommended either a coat-frock or 'coat and skirt with neat blouse beneath' for business dress. As Catherine Horwood notes in *Keeping up Appearances*, following the hierarchical etiquette that existed in many offices between the wars, typically the skilled shorthand typist or secretary favoured a formal flannel or serge suit, a regular typist usually wearing a dark frock or skirt and white blouse. Women in clerical positions not directly in the public eye dressed smartly and modestly, their appearance not usually

Postcard photograph, early 1930s.

prescribed. Otherwise many workplaces had detailed lists of 'correct' or, more commonly, 'incorrect' office wear; for instance, some companies prohibited jewellery and bright colours or short sleeves, even in summer. Hands, gloves and stockings should be flawless and shoes immaculate; but to over-dress for the office was to risk appearing low-bred, or desperate for advancement.

A popular inter-war publication that frequently featured office wear, *Miss Modern* magazine, advised in October 1930:

> Remember that appearances reveal more than they hide – and that a lost button may mean a lost job…. Wear a costume that fits you and look trim and spruce. Choose the hat that suits you best, letting it frame your face, not smother it…. Above all, avoid that Christmas-tree look. Noisy blobs of ornaments are not only distracting; they suggest you have the wrong sort of mind for business life.

Women must often have struggled to balance a natural interest in fashion and desire for femininity, with the requirement to appear neat and businesslike. With female clerical wages far below those of men, dressing well for work was not cheap either, and budgets were stretched further during the Second World War, when clothes were rationed, all resources scarce. However, perhaps the restricted, uniform-like, utility wartime look, enlivened with a glamorous hairstyle and jaunty hat, was in some respects more egalitarian, easier to achieve.

Chapter 4

Work Wear: Occupational Uniforms

Standardised Dress

As urban-industrial society grew more firmly established and Britain's population soared, many new occupations arose, while existing jobs became more structured and refined. Recognisable, homogeneous forms of dress helped to create visual order in an increasingly chaotic, crowded and anonymous world, identifying who did what, for instance on the railways, omnibuses and trams, and who to ask for help in the street, or service in a shop. During the nineteenth and early-twentieth century, standardised civilian or occupational uniforms (as distinct from military uniforms) were commonly issued to public servants including firefighters, police, postal workers and nursing staff, and to transport workers: railway employees, bus and tram crews.

'Official' employee uniforms usually comprised one or more sets of distinctive clothes fashioned in pre-determined colours to a specified pattern, outdoor uniforms often including seasonal variants. Many garments were decorated with button, lapel and cap-badge insignia representing the parent company or organisation, also displaying personal letters or numbers unique to the wearer. Uniform garments loosely followed the lines of regular dress, yet avoided high fashion features, producing a rational, businesslike image; some absorbed military details, like the belted tunic of the Victorian fireman and policeman. The style of regulation dress of different occupations typically resembled that of others at any given time, reflecting general trends in uniform design. However, headgear varied widely, and in some roles special safety helmets and other protective items were included in the kit.

When smart uniforms or 'livery' (the correct term in certain occupations) were provided as part of the employment package, this gave many of our ancestors a better working outfit than they could have provided themselves, also enabling preservation of personal clothes for 'Sunday best' and home wear (see Chapter 5). Arguably, compulsory regulation uniforms attempted to impose control, even discipline over workers, suppressing individuality and even attempting to shape characters. No doubt some of our ancestors disliked wearing identical clothes to their co-workers, or being 'labelled' through their dress, but others considered company uniforms a perk: good quality tailored suits, gleaming buttons and impressive helmets or caps could engender a sense of pride, fostering a positive work ethic and *esprit de corps*.

The complex individual histories of the various civilian or occupational uniforms worn between 1800 and 1950 are too lengthy to cover here: descriptions and illustrations feature in my *British Working Dress: Occupational Clothing, 1750–1950* (Shire, 2012). Apart from nurses and domestic servants, very few females wore uniform dress until the First World War; then mothers, sisters and daughters took over many jobs vacated by their menfolk and for the first time in British history millions of women wore occupational uniforms.

Since the mid- to late 1800s some women and men have worn closely prescribed clothes with a standardised appearance, for example in the retail and service industries. This chapter focuses on the livery and quasi-uniforms worn by domestic servants and by shop staff – two major occupations during our period.

Domestic Servants

Many of our ancestors and more recent relatives were in service, among the staff in a large establishment, or as general menservants or maids in smaller homes. Their clothes broadly reflected the division of labour within the household and their individual position within the servant hierarchy.

(i) Livery suits
Superior male servants, namely house stewards, butlers and valets, generally followed contemporary fashion in formal daywear and evening dress, depending on the time of day and occasion. During the nineteenth century, they progressed from knee breeches to trousers and over time adopted fashionable forms of coat, but generally cultivated a traditional image, their appearance lagging respectfully behind that of their master. Conversely, the lower menservants including footmen, porters, coachmen, grooms and postilions in prestigious households – mainly public-facing staff – were typically provided with picturesque uniforms known as livery suits.

Servants' livery fashioned in the family colours with heraldic crest embroidered on the coat originally derived from medieval custom, but experienced a major revival in the expanding cities of Georgian Britain. In the 1700s, livery, styled on contemporary formal dress, comprised silk or velvet coat, waistcoat, breeches, stockings, buckled shoes, powdered wig and beaver hat. The turned-down coat collar and turned-back cuffs were usually faced with a contrasting colour, garments further ornamented with silver or gold lace and fringing. In some households such elaborate livery was worn only between noon and early evening, that is, during social visiting hours or when guests

Evening guest, footman and butler: illustration from *Mrs Perkins's Ball* by W.M. Thackeray, 1847.

were entertained; otherwise footmen and other lower servants wore plain frock coats and aprons when undertaking more mundane downstairs duties. Precise arrangements concerning provision of clothing varied: often two different livery suits – everyday and more formal evening suits – were provided, the servant then buying his own shoes, linen, stockings and wig out of his wages.

By 1800, lower servants' elaborate dress was becoming a 'fossilised', archaic costume. Diverging increasingly from regular male fashion that favoured a discreet crisp tailored image, or plainer 'country' look, colourful, sumptuous richly trimmed livery suits now resembled old aristocratic modes and formal court dress. As such, they were regarded as an even more important demonstration of a family's affluence and social position within the shifting society of nineteenth-century industrial Britain. Whereas in old landowning families, livery colours were a time-honoured tradition, *nouveaux riches* households often invented garish 'family colours' for their retainers.

In prosperous Victorian homes usually only indoor footmen received rich braided coats, knee breeches, fine white stockings and buckled shoes or flat pumps, although sometimes the butler, coachmen and postilions were dressed in similar fashion. However, by the early 1900s, while ornate Georgian-style livery might still be provided in aristocratic residences, elsewhere the growing trend was for a more dignified effect. Butlers typically wore a dark morning coat, plain or striped waistcoat with dark or pinstriped trousers and black tie, footmen usually tail coats, trousers and white 'Berlin' gloves; all donned white waistcoats and white bow ties for important functions, following regular evening dress etiquette.

Modest households employing one or two unclassified male servants did not supply elaborate livery, although provision of winter and summer clothing, excepting underwear and shoes, was usually part of the hiring agreement. The conservative rural manservant characteristically wore traditional knee breeches and stockings well beyond their fashionable life. Clothing could also vary with duties, for the one man might function as groom and gardener in

Cdv photograph of a London footman, 1880s.

the morning, footman and butler later in the day. When serving indoors, a late-nineteenth- or early-twentieth-century general manservant usually dressed like the butler in larger houses: a formal jacket or tail coat, dark trousers and a white apron for waiting at table.

(ii) Outdoor uniforms

In elite establishments, keeping a fashionable equipage comprising one or more carriages, horses and attendants was deemed essential, not only for transport but also for displaying prosperity and social rank. Victorian household coachmen and stable staff generally received plainer livery than indoor servants, although some coachmen had to wear extravagant laced coats and wigs for public show. Otherwise the coachman's outer garment was a capacious greatcoat with high collar and protective overlapping shoulder capes, this later being termed a 'box coat'. Beneath was worn an elegant double-breasted frock coat with tight-fitting white breeches and leather boots, the top hat sometimes displaying a ribbon cockade in the family's colours. This smart, traditional uniform continued into the twentieth century, M.W. Webb remarking in the *Heritage of Dress* (1912) that the modern coachmen:

> ... wear the tall hat, the bright buttons, doeskin breeches and top boots characteristic of the ... riding dress of the gentleman of the beginning of the 19th century.

Coachmen also received practical working garments as part of their livery, for example overall-like smocks to protect their clothes when rubbing down the horses. Under-grooms and stable-boys typically wore a loose brown jacket in the early 1800s, but by mid-century more commonly a fitted waist-length 'coatee' resembling the jockey's shirt. Victorian and early-twentieth-century grooms generally wore breeches or, by the 1890s, wide jodhpurs, with top boots, leggings or gaiters, a tailored jacket and bowler hat. Some also favoured bright-coloured waistcoats and white cravats, producing a rather dashing effect.

By the early 1900s, some prosperous families were acquiring motor cars. The first domestic chauffeurs, often coachmen, usually wore riding breeches/jodhpurs and boots or gaiters, in recognition of their equestrian heritage. The remainder of their uniform comprised a brass-buttoned tunic-style jacket, peaked driver's cap and gauntlet gloves, with a long double-breasted outer coat for inclement weather. During the 1930s, this early chauffeurs' uniform was replaced by the more modern knee-length coat and regular trousers, only the peaked cap and leather driving gloves signifying their role.

(iii) Maids' dress

By 1800, female household staff were fewer and less visible than male servants, their wages also lower. They did not receive special livery and sometimes supplied their own working garments, their clothes not usually closely prescribed. Early-nineteenth-century visitors to prestigious urban residences remarked on the stylish appearance of the typical city housemaid in good coloured gown, neat white apron, kerchief and prettily trimmed day cap. Conversely, since servants' dress tended to reflect their role and their employers' status, the hard-working general maid in a humbler home, or country maidservant, was more likely to wear a simple cotton or linen 'washing dress', with coarse kerchief, half-apron and mob cap.

As the nineteenth century advanced, more girls and young women entered service, becoming chamber, parlour, kitchen, scullery or laundry maids in large households where roles were clearly defined, although many worked alone or with one other, as maids-of-all-work. By the early-Victorian era, the usual working garment was a washable cotton dress fashioned from plain, printed, tartan or striped fabric; following fashionable trends, during the early-nineteenth century waistlines gradually lowered, skirts grew wider and caps altered shape to accommodate changing hairstyles. Clothing was also adapted to suit the task: for example, aprons were changed between duties, particularly after cleaning the grates and before making beds. Maids' work dresses were typically worn shorter than ladies' gowns, yet their style followed fashion and some servants adopted the vast crinoline frame introduced in 1856/7.

By the mid-1800s, a more uniform look was evolving; with white day caps and aprons no longer part of fashionable dress, these items progressively came to be associated with servitude. Morning work wear usually comprised a grey or lilac cotton dress, teamed with practical black stockings, coarse apron and capacious mob cap or net to contain the hair. But the custom was developing for maids to change out of their morning housework clothes into more formal outfits for the afternoons, when visitors were present. With demand now soaring for female dining-room and drawing-room servants and parlourmaids taking over footmen's waiting duties, in many households it became customary for staff to change after lunch into a smart dark gown, finer stockings and crisp white apron and cap.

For mid- to late-Victorian live-in servants, life grew increasingly regulated, standardised uniforms categorically demonstrating their subservient status. A black or

Cabinet photograph of housemaids in afternoon uniforms, late 1890s.

dark dress was usual for parlour, chamber and 'in-between' maids, accessorised with starched white cuffs, apron and cap. Initially long half-aprons predominated, but during the 1880s maids' aprons acquired a bib, their caps growing taller from mid-decade, following fashion. During the 1890s, uniforms grew more frivolous, afternoon dresses fashioned with puffed 'leg-o'-mutton' sleeves while apron bibs developed picturesque frills and shoulder straps; the white cap was now a small 'pom-pom' headdress perched high on the head, trailing long streamers for afternoon wear.

In the early-twentieth century, maids' morning work garments generally comprised a plain or print dress, apron and traditional mob cap, the latter now somewhat outmoded. By contrast, maids' afternoon uniforms continually evolved; dainty caps were worn far back on the head, smaller aprons developed a narrow V-shaped bib and dress hemlines rose to mid-low calf length during the 1910s. When war broke out, many maids left domestic service for better-paid factory jobs or other war work. Afterwards it was more difficult for employers to find live-in staff, press advertisements frequently highlighting provision of an attractive uniform as an incentive. Between the wars, maids' dress hemlines grew shorter, rising to just below the knee and, reflecting modern technology, uniforms were fashioned from blue or green easy-care rayon.

The clothing of other female servants differed from the typical maid's uniform. The housekeeper, who represented her mistress and supervised most female servants, was usually a mature woman, a large bunch of household keys at her waist symbolising her authority. Early-nineteenth-century housekeepers generally wore a cap and apron, like other maidservants, but were discontinued when these accessories gained a specifically servile image in the mid-1800s. The Victorian or Edwardian housekeeper's formal appearance aimed to distinguish her from her subordinates, her dress usually a conservative version of prevailing fashion, sober black fabric reflecting her status and position of responsibility.

The personal maid to the lady of the house was a higher servant who reported not to the housekeeper, but directly to her mistress. Ideally a young woman with some education, sewing skills and an interest in apparel, she was expected to dress neatly and stylishly, yet not appear too ornate or overly fashionable. Usually first to receive her mistress's cast-off garments and accessories, she could wear or adapt these for her own use, or send them home to her family to be remade or sold. Despite her elevated status, the lady's maid in a large household often wore a white cap and apron with her dress, like other servants (see coloured image No.2).

Nannies and nursery maids also developed a standardised Victorian uniform comprising a neat, plain dress, white apron and cap. Mrs Beeton recommended the colour grey for nannies in her seminal domestic handbook, *Household Management* (1861), and in the early-twentieth century the Astors' nanny at Cliveden House, Buckinghamshire, wore a white blouse and grey skirt in the mornings, a dark grey dress for afternoons. Nannies trained at the prestigious Norland College (established 1892) were distinguished by their light brown uniform and embroidered 'N' motif. When worn with an outdoor cape, starched cap and bibbed apron, the uniform of the late-Victorian and Edwardian nanny resembled that of the nurse.

Cooks, kitchen and scullery maids, usually 'invisible' downstairs, generally wore a plain or printed cotton dress with short sleeves, or donned washable protective sleeves and coarse apron for cooking or rough work. An overall garment covering the whole dress was sometimes worn by cooks, but strictly in the kitchen.

Behind the Counter

Many of our ancestors worked in family businesses, helping to conduct trade, fetch and deliver goods, or serving in shops. During the nineteenth century, as urban communities grew and wholesale and retail commerce advanced, the job of shop worker became a more recognised occupation. A servile and physically demanding role, yet requiring some education, the position of shop assistant was considered more prestigious in the Victorian era than factory work or domestic service.

(i) Victorian shop girls

Early-nineteenth-century counter staff were often men, including drapery store assistants catering for a largely female clientèle, but from the 1860s onwards large shops and department stores – now entering their heyday (see Chapter 8) – began to employ many more females than before. With the average mid-Victorian, middle-class housewife controlling the household budget and considered the typical customer, store managers realised that feminine sales assistants would best understand shoppers' needs. Hundreds of thousands of shop assistants, aged from 14 years and upwards, occupied the bottom rung of the 'middle-class' occupational pyramid; later in the century new opportunities in stores also began to attract independent, educated middle-class women needing to earn a living.

Reflecting the wider development of more standardised dress and work uniforms, in large urban stores and many provincial shops a formal black dress became the 'correct' mode behind the counter. A gown of black silk, fine wool or mixed fabric was often accessorised with a starched white collar and coordinating white cuffs.

'A Portable Shop Seat': illustration from *The Girls' Own Paper*, 1880.

The style of the costume generally followed prevailing fashion; ideally, shop girls should look up-to-date yet not wear extreme dress. Victorian employers often prohibited jewellery and other adornments, so that their sales girls remained unobtrusive: their appearance should not detract from the displays of merchandise. Most shop girls had to buy or make their own smart work clothes – a considerable challenge when apprentice or junior assistant wages were as little as £10–£15 per year, significantly lower than male shop workers' earnings. The store proprietor John Lewis insisted in the mid-1880s on black, uncomfortably high-necked woollen dresses, boots and black stockings for his sales girls.

Shop girls were typically young and single, often chosen from among many applicants for their tall, elegant figures, pleasing features and luxuriant hair. Some store assistants became the first live 'mannequins' (fashion models) around the turn of the twentieth century – statuesque house models selected from among the staff to demonstrate to clients the new seasonal modes. As Pamela Cox and Annabel Hobley explain in *Shopgirls: The True Story of Life Behind the Counter*, senior saleswomen, who could earn up to £60 a year, dressed more handsomely than junior assistants in finer dresses, cultivating an air of efficient, courteous elegance. Despite their professional image, young female store staff were potentially vulnerable: pretty girls on display in opulent surroundings could easily appear 'available', like the desirable goods around them.

In 1894 *The Shop Girl*, a romantic musical comedy, was first staged at London's Gaiety Theatre, shining the spotlight on the female sales assistants who were now a major workforce.

(ii) Twentieth-century counter staff

By 1900, around 250,000 women worked in shops, the number reaching 1 million by the 1960s, fuelled by the continuing success of department stores and growth of high street multiples or chain stores from the 1920s onwards. Typically women worked in areas of retail like millinery, corsetry, drapery and other fashion departments, or in furnishings, stationery shops, confectioners and fancy goods emporia. Edwardian shop wear was typically a formal dark dress, or, reflecting the contemporary fashion for separates, a crisp white blouse and black tailored skirt. Male shop assistants also had to look smart and respectable, especially if selling men's clothes and accessories. Grocers and others in the food industry wore aprons and, from the 1910s onwards, buttoned overalls, to protect their clothes and satisfy more rigorous hygiene requirements.

Between the wars, reflecting wider sartorial trends, the strictest store dress codes began to relax: for example, by the 1920s female sales assistants in Harrods wore discreet cosmetics, jewellery and attractive frocks in sage green, the inimitable Harrods' colour. At Marshall & Snelgrove after the Second World War, fashion staff saved up for sleek grey flannel 'New Look' work suits. Smart uniforms were also issued to various grades of staff in many stores, from doormen and lift attendants to delivery van drivers decked out in store livery.

Chapter 5

Dressing Up, Dressing Down

For centuries, dress has been subject to 'rules' governing the apparel appropriate for different times of the day – customs following strict social etiquette or looser guidelines. Choosing the correct clothes for the hour and occasion was a major pre-occupation for the social elite, who generally possessed large wardrobes and whose daily schedule could entail four to six costume changes. Conversely, most of our ordinary working ancestors led simpler lives and owned fewer clothes. As outlined in Chapters 3 and 4, many wore functional work garments or special occupational uniforms during the working week. Everyone who could kept aside one or more good outfits for wear to church on Sunday and on non-work days or holidays – the smarter, more fashionable ensembles popularly referred to as 'Sunday clothes'.

While decent clothes were needed for 'dressing up' on special days, at home in private it was possible to 'dress down' in ways not publicly acceptable. For privileged ancestors who did not work and often rose late, this entailed informal morning wear or other loose garments suitable for receiving relatives and intimate friends. For working men, this meant removing uncomfortable or stiff clothes at the end of the day, or adopting unpretentious casual wear on weekends. For women based at home this was everyday domestic dress – whatever a poorer woman could manage, or a middle-class woman felt comfortable with.

'Sunday Best'

By the beginning of our period, the concept of 'Sunday best' was acknowledged throughout society and understood to mean the superior clothes kept for wearing to church, on public holidays, feast days and important social or family gatherings. 'Sunday clothes' involved one, ideally two outfits that were not workwear, or other plain weekday clothes, but better quality, smarter, more fashionable garments and accessories that were deserving of public view. In *Lark Rise to Candleford*, Flora

Thompson recalled how in her Oxfordshire hamlet during the 1880s: 'Anything did for everyday wear, as long as it was clean and whole and could be covered with a decent white apron; it was the "Sunday best" that had to be just so'.

Victorian and Edwardian family photographs demonstrate how ancestors identified as domestic servants (who presumably wore morning work dresses and perhaps uniform black gowns and aprons for afternoon duties) treated themselves to silk crinoline or bustle dresses with lace collars, ornate trimmings and fashionable jewellery – fine Sunday costumes that transformed their appearance. Even if less comfortably placed financially, earlier generations usually made a concerted effort for church, where they knew that they would be seen and assessed by the whole congregation. The small community of Lark Rise cannot have been the only one in which some 'went to church to show off their best clothes and to see and criticize those of their neighbours'.

Apparent finery was, in reality, often superficial; shoes were frequently down-at-heel, yet, as Flora Thomson explained, it was the more conspicuous dress articles that mattered, like the 'tippet', described as a little shoulder cape of velvet, silk or satin with a long, dangling fringe. Following mainstream fashion, tippets, or fitted capes, were the latest trend in Lark Rise during the early 1880s: 'All the women and some of the girls had these, and they were worn proudly to church or Sunday school with a posy of roses or geraniums pinned in front.' By contrast, older folk were far less influenced by new modes, but had their own ideas about suitable attire. 'Old Sally', over 80 years old, appeared in her 'black silk' on Sundays – the weekly resurrection of sombre, outmoded, yet handsome black drapery in rural Oxfordshire that would have been mirrored in church pews up and down the country. Indeed 'Sunday best' was often black or dark-coloured, in any case, especially within poorer communities; sombre shades were always considered smart and were versatile, suitable for all occasions, including funerals and mourning (more in Chapter 7).

'Sunday best' was equally important for men. In Lark Rise, the male Sunday toilet was an elaborate affair 'which included shaving and cutting each other's hair and much puffing and splashing with buckets of water, but stopped short before lacing up boots or putting on a collar and tie...' For most, the basic requisites would have been an un-patched suit comprising clean breeches or, by the Victorian era, usually trousers teamed with a jacket, inner waistcoat or jerkin and fresh shirt.

1. 'A Woman Churning Butter' from Costume of Great Britain (1805) by W.H. Pyne.

'The Progress of the Toilet: The :ays' by James Gillray, 1810.

French Fashions.

DINNER DRESS. CARRIAGE DRESS. PROMENADE DRESS.

Published by GB Whittaker for La Belle Assemblee No 65 New Series May 1830.

3. Fashion plate from *La Belle Assemblée*, 1830.

4. Family oil portrait, 1845.

5a and 5b. Hand-coloured ambrotype photographs, late 1850s.

6. Hand-coloured cdv photograph, late 1860s.

7. Bridal fashion plate from *The Englishwoman's Domestic Magazine*, c.1872.

8. Evening fashion plate from *The Englishwoman's Domestic Magazine*, 1876.

9. Hand-coloured cdv photograph, early to mid-1880s.

765   The Welsh Farmer's Daughter.

10. Souvenir photograph of females in national Welsh costumes, late 1800s.

11. Country, Casino and Travelling Dress by
Worth, *The Queen* 1895.

12. Humorous First World War
postcard, c.1915.

13. Leach's knitting pattern,
early 1920s.

14. Advertisement for washing dolly blue product, Reckitt's Blue, c.1925.

15. Dressmaking pattern in *Film Fashionland* magazine, September 1934.

16. Government 'Make-Do and Mend' propaganda poster: Mrs Sew-and-Sew, c.1942.

17. Simpson's menswear advertisement, 1948.

A respectable starched shirt collar and tie were important, leading to easing of tight neckwear during the church sermon. A nineteenth-century alternative was a good smock-frock, among males who generally wore the rural garments. Surviving Victorian smocks suggest that country men often kept two qualities of smock – one for weekdays and another for Sundays and special occasions, the main distinctions between working and 'best' smocks being of colour, quality of fabric and quantity of embroidery.

Sundays, being special, were recalled fondly down the generations in some families. In 1867 a journeyman engineer Thomas Wright wrote: 'No man can remember a time when working men did not take a pride in having, and look upon as necessary to the proper enjoyment of the Sunday, that outward and visible sign of working class respectability and prosperity, a Sunday suit.' Evidently for some, 'Sunday best' was not simply about exhibiting a pleasant public appearance, but a significant personal and social ritual – a symbol of respectability.

The importance of a neat, respectable Sunday suit was highlighted by the shame experienced by those who did not possess suitable clothes. Victorian Poor Law commissioners' reports repeatedly noted that young apprentice farm workers (often indentured aged 9) failed to attend church for want of decent garments. In 1843, one commissioner found

Photograph of late-Edwardian celebration, showing 'Sunday best', c.1907–09.

that 'although they are sufficiently clothed for their work, they sometimes have no better kind of clothing for the Sunday; and their masters are ashamed to let them appear at church in their ordinary dress of the week.'

This was echoed a generation later when, in 1867, another commissioner's report noted how in certain menial farm jobs carried out by boys, typically '...the boy never cleans himself, never puts on his best clothes, loses all reverence for the Sabbath'. Not only did obvious want of suitable Sunday dress reflect badly on the individual, but also implied lack of due respect for God on the holiest of days; dress and respectability were intertwined with Victorian notions of morality.

In poorer households, the absence of Sunday outfits was a direct expression of poverty; there simply weren't enough decent clothes to go round the family and weekday outfits had to be worn on Sundays too. Many women struggling to manage a limited domestic budget only coped by depositing the family's Sunday clothes and other portable items in the local pawn shop during the week in return for cash, then redeeming them on Saturday afternoon or evening (when wages were paid) for wear again on Sunday. Considering the interest charged every time, using this method good clothes were paid for many times over, but as valuable commodities they saw the family through the week and preserved their dignity.

Nineteenth-century values continued into the Edwardian era in many parts of the country. In 1907 Lady Florence Bell, wife of a Middlesborough iron founder, published her investigations into local workers' living and working conditions in *At the Works,* stating that in addition to certain work clothes, all the men needed to be equipped with a Sunday best suit. Times change, however; during and after the First World War church attendance declined and as living standards rose for many, the traditional significance of special Sunday or best clothes declined. Although many working families still took pride in displaying their hard-earned 'Sunday clothes', old values were increasingly looked down upon by the upwardly mobile middle classes.

At Home

Behind closed doors, earlier generations could escape the strictures of public dress. Traditionally the upper classes rose late, slipped on a loose wrapping gown, informal unfitted gown or *peignoir* and took breakfast, read their correspondence or the newspaper and began to prepare for their day. In the early 1800s, ladies' relaxed morning indoor wear was referred to as 'Morning Dress', a dainty, concealing long-sleeved, high-necked garment of fine fabric, accessorised with picturesque day cap. This was an outfit that did not require corsetry or other rigid under-structures, enabling a leisurely, comfortable start to the day. A lady's close relatives and maidservants might view her in this modest state of 'undress', but for more formal visitors she would present a more 'dressed' appearance.

In the mid-1800s, loose indoor 'jackets' and skirts also became fashionable; these and other unshaped morning gowns were especially useful for pregnant ladies, most of whom still wore corsets (albeit sometimes modified) with regular fitted garments. Later, another mode, the delicate tea gown, evolved as informal but more alluring indoor wear.

Fashion plate from *Ackermann's Repository of Arts*, May 1816

To bridge the growing gap between luncheon and dinner, during the mid-Victorian period an afternoon 'snack' of tea, sandwiches and cake evolved. Married ladies embraced this ritual, inviting intimate friends as guests, and from the 1870s onwards began to don special tea gowns for the occasion. These were flowing, feminine dresses that could be worn with relaxed corsetry and were typically fashioned from fine silk muslin, embellished with lace and ribbons. Like many traditional customs, this fashion declined during and after the First World War, but other informal indoor modes took their place, from daring new lounging pyjamas in the 1920s and 1930s to the buttoned housecoats of the 1940s and 1950s.

For ordinary family women, especially housewives at home with children, there were no languorous lounging garments for lazy mornings or receiving afternoon visitors, merely basic workaday clothes for doing the household chores. For much of the 1800s these comprised a simple linen or cotton washing dress fashioned more or less in the prevailing style, or, from around the turn of the century, a plain blouse and dark tailored skirt. Invariably indoor clothes were covered by a large apron that not only protected them, but also concealed from view what were often old, threadbare garments. Sometimes women were photographed by street or travelling photographers, posing proudly outside their homes wearing neat workaday clothes and a fresh apron – a symbol of domestic pride when garments were in good repair.

By contrast, many poorer women whose priority was ensuring that their menfolk and children were adequately clothed neglected their own appearance to such a pitiful extent that they were virtually confined indoors, out of sight. Maud Pember Reeves' study of working-class Lambeth families, *Round About a Pound a Week* (1913) makes for sobering reading:

> The women seldom get new clothes. The men go to work and must be supplied, the children must be decent at school, but the mother has no need to appear in the light of day. If very badly equipped she can shop in the evening … and no'one will notice under her jacket and rather long skirt what she is wearing on her feet. Most of them have a hat, a jacket and a 'best' skirt to wear in the street. In the house a blouse and patched skirt under a sacking apron is the universal wear….

In the early 1800s, gentlemen often wore a loose Indian-style morning gown, traditionally termed a 'banyan' when indoors – a popular Georgian mode deriving from forms of eastern robe that early travellers had first encountered overseas. Precise styling and terminology changed over time, but for the upper and upper-middle classes the vogue for easy house gowns, often fashioned from luxurious imported materials, continued into the Regency era and beyond. Not only was it uncomfortable lounging at home in stiff, formal day clothes, but when fabrics were hard to care for, the shape of structured garments was easily ruined, so relaxed indoor gowns for men became customary for family time and receiving close friends at home.

Victorian and Edwardian gentlemen continued this practice, removing outdoor or office jacket, coats and stiff starched collars and donning a dressing- or wrapping-gown. Also popular from the mid-1800s was the shorter smoking jacket, styled like the regular male lounge jacket, but made in soft woollen or velvet material in rich colours like dark red, green and blue, or black, with quilted silk lining and cord trimmings. Jackets and longer gowns fashioned in exotic oriental fabrics or plush quilted velvet material were often accessorised with a Chinese- or Middle-Eastern-style tasselled 'smoking cap'. Smoking caps and gowns or jackets were worn ostensibly to protect the clothes and hair from the aroma of cigar or cheroot smoke, but were also luxurious, offering a sense of escapism from dreary business wear. Smoking caps were unfashionable by the turn of the century but comfortable smoking jackets remained customary for casual or semi-formal wear at home in the evenings, teamed with ordinary day or evening trousers. In 1956, Austin Reed

Fashion plate detail from *The Gazette of Fashion*, January 1857.

launched a modern version of the smoking jacket, the 'Television Jacket', in wine velour with quilted collar and cuffs.

Many of the ordinary working men in our families would have arrived home from work, discarding jackets, perhaps waistcoats, also removing starched shirt collar (if worn), sometimes rolling up sleeves and little bothered by genteel dress codes that declared it indecent to bare the arms, or reveal the trouser braces. Stiff leather boots or laced shoes were replaced with cosy slippers indoors; in middle-class households men would take care not to display their sock suspenders when sitting down and changing their footwear. To show garment fastenings usually hidden, even at home, was considered unseemly in status-conscious early-twentieth-century households.

Older, conservative men often felt awkward when not wearing a formal three-piece suit, even indoors, but increasingly younger males felt confined in the evenings and at weekends in tailored suits redolent of the office. As knitwear became established in the regular wardrobe, easy-to-wear buttoned cardigans, jerseys and pullovers came into their own for relaxed wear at home, many men having a stretchy 'vest' or slip-over knitted for them, replacing the tailored waistcoat. Comfortable knitted garments of the 1920s to 1940s could be plain-coloured, striped or intricately patterned, like the Argyle and Fair Isle designs becoming fashionable for golf. Knitted sweaters and vests were often teamed with grey flannel trousers or wide plus fours, loose knickerbockers that billowed over the top of the socks. Plus fours were also worn for sports (see Chapter 6) but proved useful all-round weekend clothes. Some men also wore them for gardening – the new hobby that followed the interwar surge in home ownership and suburban living.

Between the wars almost 3 million newly built homes were purchased by private buyers. Many families were trying to 'better themselves' with their first house and the pressure was on to 'keep up with the Joneses'. Few married women went out to work, most housewives spending their day running the home and caring for children. Many set high standards of domesticity and of dress, unlike earlier generations of mothers when some had been too poor or exhausted to take pride in their appearance. Decent frocks were often worn at home with a tidy apron or overall for doing the housework, quickly removed if the front doorbell rang. Some women developed a habit of wearing older clothes in the morning, changing into better garments after lunch. Trousers were not in common use until after the 1950s, so relaxed slacks were rare indoors and a respectable dress or blouse and skirt were the norm.

Snapshot photograph, late 1930s.

Holiday Clothes

Due to nineteenth-century changes in the workplace, gradually there evolved more designated periods of leisure time away from business and the concept of the holiday as a relaxing break. The development of industrial society generated a growing need for rest periods, a change of scenery and fresh air. At the height of summer, the metropolis felt stifling, crowded and grimy, and among the financially well-placed there arose the custom of migrating to the countryside or the coast. Initially holidays were beyond the means of many of our working forebears – an indulgence for those with money and time at their disposal. However, from the mid-1800s onwards, with the expansion of railway networks offering affordable fares, better provision of paid leave in some industries, and the Bank Holidays Act of 1871, more workers and their families could enjoy a modest break in Britain – a day trip, long weekend or even a week's vacation.

The late-Georgian wealthy classes either frequented elegant spa towns or burgeoning coastal resorts – fashionable social hubs like Brighton, Cheltenham, Bath and Scarborough, with promenades, assembly rooms and theatres – or ventured on to unspoilt moors and mountains seeking the dramatic, picturesque scenery so beloved of the Romantic poets. Stout clothes, often warm, older items such as woollen cloaks and greatcoats tended to be worn for travelling and the outdoors. Some ladies adopted fashionable tailored riding habit-style costumes, while finer, more formal apparel was reserved for promenading or attending indoor entertainments. A major change occurred in the mid-nineteenth century, when travelling in Britain (and overseas) became more organised, with firms like Thomas Cook's offering escorted excursions from the 1840s – effectively the world's first 'package tours'. The time was now ripe for robust outfits appropriate for railway travel and steamship voyages, and the introduction of dedicated holiday clothes.

As Penelope Byrde explains in *Nineteenth Century Fashion*, as travel and tourism advanced, women's middle-class periodicals started to feature fashions for journeys and holidays, while etiquette books advised a new generation of tourists and holidaymakers on how to behave and dress when on the move or staying in hotels and lodgings. Vacations were seen as a time for relaxation, ease, a degree of outdoor exercise and even romance. Accordingly, holiday attire should be comfortable, functional and attractive – based on contemporary fashion, but adapted for the special circumstances. Travelling clothes needed to be able to cope with dust, dirt and creasing, while the outfits brought away and unpacked on arrival had to cover both daytime leisure wear and evening diversions (for more on evening wear, see Chapter 7).

During the later 1850s and 1860s, the prevailing silhouette for both sexes was wide and bulky, and comfortable unshaped clothes were well adapted to informal outdoor wear. For men, the loose lounging jacket with useful outside pocket was a welcome innovation, teamed with wide-cut lightweight trousers or tailored in tweed and worn with full knickerbockers for the countryside. For women, an early form of blouse developed c.1860; sometimes styled with a masculine shirt collar and bow tie, or in red wool in the loose 'Garibaldi' style, this became a popular mode for walking when matched with short, loose-fitting jacket and wide crinoline skirt. For travelling and walking, skirts at this time were made short, without trains, the hem well off the floor or looped-up, and worn over a coloured petticoat (underskirt) and bright stockings. Knitted cotton 'Balybriggan stockings' were recommended for the country, as worn by the Queen, a popular style of outdoor boot the 'Balmoral', named after the royal family's Scottish holiday home.

Fresh air and sunshine were invigorating benefits of holidays and open-air excursions, but freckles and sunburn were not favoured in genteel circles, being associated with outdoor manual labour. Various wide-

Ryde Pier, Isle of Wight, the *Illustrated London News*, 1859.

brimmed straw hats evolved for men, women and children for wear at the seaside; typically ribbon-trimmed like sailors' hats, these effectively shielded the face from harmful rays. Parasols were also widely used for added shade, a picturesque accessory to be carried, but also useful for propping up as a sunshade on the beach.

Many mid-century visitors to the seaside did not venture into the sea, but those taking a dip used horse-drawn bathing machines. These were wheeled changing huts, drawn out into the water by horses, with pegs and benches inside for storing regular clothes, and steps at the far end for entering the water, suitably attired. Traditionally men and boys usually swam naked, but on most public Victorian beaches this was officially prohibited, so males sometimes donned rudimentary bathing trunks. Many disliked the woollen drawers, which easily filled with water and were not as modest as intended. By the 1870s, a close-fitting, leotard-like one-piece costume had developed for men, with top and drawers combined – better suited to energetic male swimming. Towards 1900 the sleeves and legs of men's costumes grew briefer and bold striped fabric came into vogue.

During the mid- to late-nineteenth century, there were close links between holiday clothes and sports wear (covered separately in Chapter 6). Besides broadly reflecting prevailing aesthetic taste and being of acceptable appearance, both had to be functional and comfortable, providing ease of movement. Sport and holidays each offered an informal environment permitting relaxation of some of the constraints of formal behaviour and fashionable dress, and these became the main arenas in which new sartorial ideas were trialled. A prime example is the controversial concept of Victorian women wearing bifurcated garments – bloomers or trousers. Promoted by early feminists and dress reformers including Amelia Bloomer, these met with little success when introduced as regular day dress; instead, suitably modified, they became a solution to some of the practical requirements of women's leisure activities and sports, including beachwear.

By the 1860s, when travel to the coast and seaside holidays were reaching new heights, fashion plates were promoting new styles of two-piece female bathing costumes, more structured than the shapeless linen gowns previously worn by leisured ladies when taking the waters. One variant was the knee-length flannel or serge 'paletot' dress with a full skirt, worn over bloomer-style pants; the other a shorter, belted hip-length tunic teamed with loose trousers. A linen or oiled silk bathing cap protected delicate heads from the cold, while a wide-brimmed hat on top provided shade from the sun. These trouser or bloomer bathing costumes were considered attractive and since most Victorian ladies merely bobbed around in the water, advances in female swimwear were gradual, characterised by a shortening of garments towards the century's close.

Seaside holiday clothes became lighter and more relaxed during the 1890s and early 1900s. Women's summer wear comprised serge or linen skirts and short jackets, worn with a light blouse, while men adopted pale flannels and striped blazers resembling popular sports wear. Both sexes favoured the lightweight straw boater hat around the turn of the century; for women this was a brief vogue, but men's boaters remained fashionable until the 1920s. Meanwhile, Edwardian beaches were packed with day-trippers and holidaymakers; mixed bathing grew common and more families enjoyed the water, paddling with clothes hitched up or bathing further out in modern swimsuits. Women's cumbersome bathing ensembles were slimming down, a belted dress or tunic with fashionable sailor-style collar often teamed with knee-length drawers or stockings and pumps, and topped with cap or turban-style scarf. Athletic sports were advancing rapidly and with a new generation of young women now entering serious competitive swimming, a more streamlined fitted costume with thigh-length legs developed; called the 'unitard', this sleek, body-hugging style was considered too daring by the average holidaymaker until after the First World War.

During the early 1920s, some women preferred traditional concealing two-piece bathing suits, although garments steadily contracted, the tunic neckline lowering, sleeves reducing to broad shoulder straps and hemlines rising, the drawers becoming thigh-length shorts. Increasingly the traditional thick serge or woollen cloth layers seemed a hindrance and, as reservations about revealing bodily contours progressively relaxed, the once-controversial one-piece female 'unitard' costume or *maillot*, similar to men's swimwear, gained favour. These costumes became especially close-fitting when stretchy cotton and woollen jersey fabrics began to be used during the 1920s; they were often striped, or had sporty coloured trims, while rubber bathing caps (ideal for newly bobbed hair) and rubber two-tone beach shoes came into vogue.

From the late 1920s, suntans were deemed desirable in Britain, now that tanned, glowing skin implied leisure rather than outdoor manual toil. Accordingly, summer beachwear and swimming costumes began

Snapshot photograph, North Devon, 1924.

to reveal more flesh; new short sun dresses with thin shoulder straps became fashionable, sets of beach 'pyjamas' comprising halter-neck top or sleeveless blouse and wide-legged trousers a late 1920s/early 1930s' trend. Modern female swimwear featured low backs, cut-away sides, narrow shoulder straps or halter-necklines, legs of costumes now high thigh-length, the hips fitted with a modesty skirt. Elasticated synthetic fabric such as lastex began to be used, although jersey material was still common at this date. Sleek, athletic costumes were well-suited to the new interest in health and physical fitness, the 1930s also witnessing the proliferation of public outdoor lidos for swimming and sunbathing.

Men's costumes generally retained a sleeveless vest section until around mid-decade, after which short-legged trunks grew more common, webbing waist belts giving a tailored effect. The year 1946 marked the official unveiling of the daring two-piece female bikini that bared the midriff (named after Bikini Atoll in the Pacific), although versions had been worn since c.1929. Many women found the skimpier post-war bikini too risqué, but the glamorous corseted swimsuits of the 1940s and 1950s, featuring shaped stomach panels, boning and bra cups were seen as alluring. After the Second World War, as beaches reopened, printed cotton sundresses and playsuits (with shorts) became fashionable for women, while for general beachwear and holiday wear, men finally settled in to wearing more casual clothes that freed the limbs. Open-necked, short-sleeved sports shirts and shorts were comfortable, practical garments that reflected the principles of the Men's Dress Reform Party (1929–40), who had been campaigning for more rational menswear.

The fashion for sunbathing as an accompaniment to swimming and development of holiday clothes, as experienced by our more recent relatives, prompted other new accessories. Cool, open sandals, worn by children with bare legs from the 1920s, became more common among men and women in the 1930s, worn with or without socks. Dark sunglasses, described occasionally in overseas travel writings from the early 1800s onwards as necessary protection from glare and dust, came into more general use during the 1930s. Early shades were usually circular with steel or white plastic rims, growing more glamorous during the 1940s and 1950s, with wing-shaped lenses and bright-coloured frames. Homemade nose shields were a common sight – often a fold of newspaper secured under the nose-piece of the glasses. Suntan lotion was widely used by the 1940s, but more commonly for its bronzing effect than as a sun screen; early tanning products from the likes of Nivea and Elizabeth Arden were essentially basting oils or creams without useful sun protection factors.

Family snapshot,
Worthing, August
1935.

Chapter 6

Sports Wear

P articipating in outdoor sports offered past generations a rare opportunity to take active physical exercise and escape the constraints of regular life. Horse-riding for pleasure was an elite pursuit long-enjoyed by men and women; otherwise energetic activities were mainly male-dominated in the early 1800s, including boxing, early team games such as cricket and rowing. Victorian ladies might engage in the genteel pastimes of archery and croquet, but only in the late-nineteenth and early-twentieth centuries did new, more inclusive forms of recreation develop. With advancing ideas about health and fitness and increasing female determination to experience greater social freedom, women learned to play tennis and golf, ride bicycles, drive motorcars and go walking, hiking and rambling. Reflecting these developments, looser, more comfortable clothes and dedicated sports gear gradually appeared in ordinary wardrobes. Here we look at the evolution of dress worn for some of the key sports that ancestors and more recent relatives may have enjoyed.

Horse-Riding

Horseback riding was a primary mode of transport in the pre-mechanised age, as well as a middle- and upper-class leisure activity, including the now-controversial practice of hunting. Equestrian skills being traditionally taught as part of a genteel education, competence in the saddle was considered an important accomplishment, as well as a practical expedient. Riding could involve men, women and children and in early times there were only minor distinctions between riding dress and everyday wear.

In the early 1800s, men's riding attire closely resembled stylish male daywear for, as outlined in Chapter 1, the sporting 'country' look was a dominant influence on male fashion. An immaculate, tailed riding-coat worn with well-fitting breeches or pantaloons, leather-top boots, fine linen neckwear and stylish brimmed hat was both recognised country wear of the late-Georgian aristocracy and gentry, and the favoured mode for display of sartorial style and horsemanship by fashionable men about town. However, as regular daywear evolved into a sober industrial 'uniform', riding dress began to appear more distinctive. The early-Victorian horseman teamed trousers or tight-fitting pantaloons with a waistcoat and 'Newmarket' coat (with sloping front skirts), or frock coat. During the 1850s, a looser, fuller-skirted 'Doncaster' coat appeared, but eventually racing-inspired names largely gave way to the term 'morning' coat (since gentlemen generally rode in the mornings). Trousers and morning coat remained correct for riding in town, while for the country new-style breeches developed during the 1860s and 1870s, worn with gaiters and ankle boots.

The comfortable lounge jacket, popular for everyday wear, now also began to be used on horseback, usually featuring a special back-vent and teamed with breeches. Riding breeches with long boots became popular again, but now as dedicated equestrian dress. Shaped full to the knee and often 'strapped' with leather inside the thighs, wide jodhpur-style breeches – devised initially for polo in India – were fashionable by the 1890s, teamed with lounge jacket or morning coat. The smart late-Victorian rider also wore a waistcoat, shirt, collar and tie, top hat or bowler, or, from the 1890s, the soft cloth cap. A similar ensemble, comprising tailored lounge-style hacking jacket, jodhpurs, hat/cap or peaked jockey-style riding cap, effectively became 'fossilised' riding dress during the early to mid-1900s, more formal attire reserved for classic equestrian events including dressage and hunting.

By 1800, women who rode horseback were well accustomed to adopting a special riding ensemble or 'habit' – a feminised version of male dress and the only ladies clothing then made by a male tailor. A plain, yet stylish costume also adopted for fashionable promenade and travelling dress, when used for riding the substantial habit followed contemporary fashion, with modifications. The early-nineteenth-century neo-classical habit comprised a short spencer jacket and matching skirt worn over a high-necked, short-waist blouse or 'habit shirt', or long pelisse-style coat-like garment – both accessorised with leather gloves and a masculine-style hat. Late-Georgian women's riding attire often incorporated military features, reflecting ongoing wars with France. Expressed in military-style braiding ('frogging') and plumed peaked caps or helmet-like headwear, these added a dashing, martial air to the appearance of active ladies on horseback, often dubbed 'amazons'.

Early-Victorian habits generally comprised a tailored coat or jacket with short *basque* or peplum (short skirt-like section or flounce attached to the waist), the collar and lapels opening out over a plain habit-shirt and masculine necktie. Picturesque cavalier-style feathered hats were fashionable and, following general dress trends, the skirt was now full, with a dangerously long train. Although unseen beneath the skirt, for comfort and modesty some women wore cotton pantaloons strapped under the foot. When riding progressed as a female recreation in the mid-1800s, stouter trousers of cloth or chamois leather began to replace the flimsy pantaloons; pioneering bifurcated garments for women, eventually these were fashioned from knee downwards in material to match the habit skirt.

Predictably, the cumbersome crinoline and bustle were not worn on horseback; indeed, subverting wider fashion, habit skirts grew more slender during the 1860s and 1870s, serious horsewomen favouring a plain, dark-coloured habit with top hat and veil. In 1875, the 'safety' skirt was invented, featuring a back slit worn open when mounted, reducing the risk of an unseated rider becoming entangled in her skirt. Habit tailoring grew progressively more complex, the two sides of the skirt differing following the addition of a third pommel to the side-saddle: this

Country-house album photograph c.1868–71.

affected the 'sit' of the skirt, prompting pouch-like shaping for the right knee. Eventually, in the later 1910s and 1920s, horsewomen began to ride astride in male fashion, discarding traditional skirts, except for traditional events. A practical jacket with riding breeches or jodhpurs and bowler hat or peaked riding hat presented a more uniform image among male and female riders between the wars and in the mid-twentieth century.

Tennis

Lawn tennis developed from the 1870s as a leisure and social pursuit, initially among the privileged classes, who played for amusement in country house gardens and private indoor courts. The new sport rapidly gained momentum, being included in the activities of The All England Croquet Club in Wimbledon in 1875, followed by the inaugural (men-only) Lawn Tennis Championships in 1877 and ladies' events from 1884. Local tennis clubs proliferated in late-Victorian and Edwardian England and public tennis courts appeared in municipal parks. The teaching of tennis in school began in elite institutions, expanding considerably between the wars. On most courts there were no official dress 'rules' (Wimbledon's 'almost entirely white' dress code dates from 1963), so when choosing what to wear, players tried to balance comfort with propriety – issues that applied to many strenuous sports.

Early male tennis players enjoyed some freedom from regular dress, wearing clothes resembling those already in use for sports like cricket. During the 1870s generally, a loose white shirt was teamed with trousers or knickerbockers and stockings, a lounge jacket typically worn at the start of a game, but often discarded during play. In the 1880s, some players adopted striped sports' shirts or crew-necked woollen jerseys; by late decade, white flannel trousers were usual, worn with soft, rubber-soled canvas shoes. During the 1890s, a plain or striped flannel blazer became fashionable, often teamed with a round sportsman's cap, the blazer pocket bearing the wearer's club badge.

Edwardian tennis players usually wore white or cream flannel suits with shirts and ties. In 1908 the *Tailor and Cutter* advertised a

> ...flannel suit ... made easy fitting at all parts and without lining.... Trousers are ... easy fitting and of full length as they will frequently have to stand cleaning, which is sure to shrink them.... The vest [waistcoat] is an optional part of this suit.

Styles changed little between the early 1900s and the late 1920s, when finally men's dress at large grew more relaxed, a casual open-necked shirt replacing the formal collar and tie. By the early 1930s, short-sleeved sports' shirts were growing acceptable, an even more daring development also occurring. In 1933, Bunny Austin was the first male player to enter a major public competition wearing not trousers, but shorts. His lead soon followed by others, he was also championed by the Men's Dress Reform Party, who had already been advocating shorts for sports and leisure wear. For some time shorts and long trousers co-existed on the courts, shorts becoming the favoured option by the Second World War.

Unlike men, female players were governed principally by fashion and in the later 1870s wore the figure-hugging 'Princess' gown. Thick flannel, jersey and serge materials were customary for early tennis costumes, although when Maud Watson became the first Wimbledon Ladies' champion in 1884, pale-coloured or white garments were already popular, as they helped to mask the dreaded perspiration. Pinafores with ball pockets were also a useful addition at this time. In 1885, *The Field* magazine recommended: 'A costume of pale blue flannel with deep kilted skirt and long basque bodice, an embroidered apron with pocket to hold the balls....'

Otherwise ladies' tennis dress displayed conventional dress features, even the cumbersome projecting bustle during the mid- to late 1880s.

Unidentified print dated 1879.

The National Dress Society (later renamed the Rational Dress Society) advocated more appropriate garments, suggesting the removal of hampering corsets and even adoption of a practical bloomer costume. However, female bloomers resembling men's knickerbockers were generally considered unattractive and scarcely worn for tennis. This was also true of the 'comfortable divided skirts', or curious 'expanding dress' proposed by health writer Ada Ballin in *The Science of Dress* (1885). Concerns about appearing 'unladylike' delayed any real progress in the development of Victorian female tennis attire, fashion periodicals continuing to endorse coquettish, feminine costumes. At the century's close, Lottie Dod, Wimbledon champion during the late 1880s and 1890s, yearned for 'a suitable attire for women's tennis which does not impede breathing'.

Edwardian women's tennis dress continued to follow fashion, the separate blouse and skirt ensemble widely worn in the early 1900s proving more comfortable than fitted Victorian gowns. Hemlines also began to be worn several inches off the ground, enabling slightly easier movement. In 1905, American tennis player May Sutton shocked Wimbledon by rolling back her cuffs to reveal her elbows, her sleeves 'too long and too hot'; this bold move helped to further the concept of freeing limbs from constricting garments.

In the early-twentieth century, white became firmly established for women's tennis dress. *Our Home* magazine wrote on 1 July 1911:

> Every year there is a discussion as to what is best to play in, but every year the question arrives at the same answer. The short, fairly full, white linen skirt is the best from all points of view, and the white silk shirt.

These garments were underlined with one or more thick petticoats and knee-length knickers – substantial layers that ensured the light did not shine through, immodestly revealing the player's silhouette.

Women's tennis wear was revolutionised when Frenchwoman Suzanne Lenglen played Wimbledon after the First World War, wearing a flimsy un-corseted short-sleeved, calf-length cotton frock, with a length of silk chiffon as a makeshift headband. Dresses rose to the knee in the late 1920s, by which time Californian Helen Wills Moody had also introduced the golf-style visor as a practical and stylish tennis accessory. During the 1930s, divided skirts resembling culottes were introduced, the prototype of female 'shorts'. Initially a debate raged over these garments, but by late decade, tailored shorts and short-sleeved shirts were an acceptable alternative to short pleated skirts and dresses.

Cycling

Various pedal-powered 'velocipedes' were trialled in the nineteenth century and when the first sporting and social cycling clubs formed in the late 1870s and 1880s, daring young men rode the towering 'high-wheel' or 'penny-farthing', while more cautious gentlemen and ladies favoured lower, less risky tricycles. In 1885, the first successful 'safety' bicycle was developed, having all the basic components of modern bikes. This encouraged more people to try the sport and when fully functioning pneumatic tyres were added in the early 1890s, cycling as a leisure pursuit rapidly gained popularity. While bicycles were easily affordable for our wealthier late-Victorian ancestors, some young working men and women also enjoyed the sport, hiring or saving up for their own machines and enjoying mixed bicycling excursions.

When cycling grew fashionable in the late-Victorian era, men usually wore knee-breeches or knickerbockers with stockings, woollen or flannel shirt and jacket or knitted woollen jersey – a stretchy garment popular with sportsmen. Soft heelless shoes were introduced especially for cycling, casual cloth caps the usual headgear, the cap or a jacket lapel often displaying a cycling club badge. Similar kit was worn in the early

Chelmsford Bicycle Club, 1895.

1900s, but significant changes occurred between the wars, when bicycles and tandems became mass-produced and therefore affordable for many more ordinary people. By the 1930s, open-necked, short-sleeved sports shirts, cool linen jackets, tailored shorts and knee socks were worn for weekend and holiday cycling, entrants in competitive cycle races wearing sporty striped cycling jerseys.

For early female cyclists, sensible, functional garments were recommended, especially by dress reformers concerned about health and comfort. In *Tips for Cyclists* (1887), Professor Hoffman drew attention to the Sanitary Woollen Company, which:

> ...cater in great variety for ladies, and among their specialities will be found woollen corsets, a great boon to ladies who insist on cycling in such a garment.... It is hardly necessary to remark that anything like tight lacing must be strictly avoided.

Most women cycled in a plain tailored jacket (removed when needed), blouse and skirt, the hemline worn around ankle-length or pinned up when in the saddle. By the mid-1890s, some were boldly adopting bifurcated garments referred to as 'rationals' – wide knee-length knickerbockers or 'bloomers', teamed with stockings and shoes. One pioneer was 16-year-old Tessie Reynolds, who in September 1893 wore cycling rationals when she rode a man's racing bicycle from Brighton to London and back in a record-breaking 8½ hours. Her father, a Brighton bicycle dealer, athletics coach and PE instructor, had encouraged Tessie to wear knickerbockers for serious cycling, her sister helping to tailor her costume and the pattern afterwards lent to members of the Brighton Ladies' Cycling Club, who all wore rationals by 1894. Mr Reynolds was exceptionally modern; many men disliked seeing women in male clothing, regarding rationals, like cycling itself, as symbolic of female emancipation.

Cycling as a means of transport or weekend pursuit gave many Victorian and Edwardian women a new sense of physical and social freedom, while also helping to advance the principles of rational dress and general clothing reform. As cycling became a mass pursuit between the wars, a new generation of female cyclists wore shorts, short-sleeved sports shirts and lightweight jackets on bicycles and tandems. Now that it was acceptable to reveal the limbs and fashionable to gain a suntan, they also wore ankle socks, popular for adult female sports, from cycling and tennis to golf and hiking.

Snapshot photograph, Isle of Wight, dated 1941.

Motoring

Following the advent of the automobile in the 1890s, motoring grew fashionable among the wealthy of Edwardian Britain. Early motor cars, without windscreen or windows, were open to the elements and motorists sat firmly *on* the vehicle, fully exposed to view. Motoring therefore not only demanded new kinds of protective outerwear but also created another occasion for sartorial display. Novel lines of purpose-designed clothing and accessories rapidly evolved, from car rugs and overcoats to boots and gauntlets. Some items were more functional than fashionable, but from the outset motoring expressed affluence and privilege, linking motoring with prestige and style.

Despite the glamour of motoring, driving in open cars in all weathers could be hazardous. The new sport required heavy-duty protective clothing and early gear was available from long-established manufacturers of quality outerwear. Aquascutum (established 1851) and Burberry (1856) were both pioneers of stout, water-resistant fabrics, already used by sportsmen and for certain occupations. Later, in 1893, Alfred Dunhill launched 'Dunhill's Motorities', items including leather overcoats, goggles, time pieces and other accessories, while department stores like Gamages began to stock everything for the fashionable motorist. Early drivers and passengers had to dress according to the weather and motoring coats were available in various materials. Long, loose-fitting waterproofed motoring coats were essential, with Burberry's 'Viator' and 'Rusitor' both popular Edwardian styles, while tweed and Irish frieze provided some of the warmest woollen coats. Many male motorists favoured a caped Ulster overcoat, a sturdy Victorian garment, often fur-lined for driving.

Fur coats were already luxury status symbols and motoring also encouraged adoption of other, previously unfashionable animal skins. A new range of men's fur coats, shaggy and consciously primitive-looking, included goat, bear, wolf, jackal and racoon, these bulky, rugged garments remaining popular for driving open-topped sports cars even when closed automobiles grew more commonplace during the 1920s. Ladies' fur and leather motoring coats were designed for comfort and style, Russian pony skin coats and suits of warm, lightweight Danish kid much admired.

In the early 1900s, many roads were unpaved, especially in rural areas, and in dry weather dust clouds hampered vision and breathing, and covered motorists' clothes. Summer motorists often wore a loose-fitting lightweight dust or duster coat of unlined canvas, linen, flannel or alpaca, usually off-white, grey or beige, with sleeves featuring elasticated or strapped inner cuffs. Protective headgear ranged from peaked driving caps and conventional cloth caps to deerstalkers and other ear-flapped hats. Some women adopted peaked caps, although a hat and veil became more usual, to screen hair and face from dust and oil smuts and protect the complexion. Adjustable gauze veils, worn up or drawn down over the face, were layered over a fashionable wide-brimmed hat and tied under the chin, an extra veil of rubber tissue kept handy, for use in sudden rain. More functional headwear that preserved a good hat or ornate hairstyle included wire-framed hoods covered with stout veiling and incorporating a mica window at eye level, bizarrely resembling bee-keepers' hoods.

Driving on un-made roads without a windscreen also exposed motorists to flying debris like loose stones, horseshoe nails and insects. To shield the eyes, male drivers generally used goggles of various types, including convex nickel- or aluminium-rimmed eye-glasses on an elastic strap, or a one-piece mica mask or eye-shield. Dedicated motoring goggles set into a close-fitting leather mask afforded the best protection and in winter these also shielded the eyes from cold air, which, along with other irritants, caused eye infections. Although most women preferred veils, some used goggles, especially serious motorists who drove at speed. Other early accessories included warm fur car rugs and goats' hair or fur-lined leather foot muffs and foot protectors, some made all-in-one with lap robes to wrap around the body. Protective driving gloves or gauntlets with long stiffened cuffs in leather or fur were both practical and fashionable.

Dorothy Levitt (1882–1922), pioneering motorist and reportedly the first British woman to win a race, held firm opinions about female motoring dress and accessories. In her manual for lady drivers, *The Woman and the Car* (1909), she advised against wearing woollen

Postcard photograph, c.1905.

gloves, favouring good, soft kid-leather. Her suggestion that gloves and other personal items like handkerchief and veil could be kept 'in the little drawer under the seat of the car' probably inspired the development of the 'glove compartment' in later vehicles. Another tip was to keep handy a vanity mirror, not simply for beauty purposes, but as a rear-view driving mirror, before cars were built with these attachments. Her recommendations reflected the dual considerations of early motoring gear: practical demands and presenting a fine figure at the wheel.

By the late 1920s, modern motorcars tended to be enclosed, lessening the need for special protective dress, although streamlined open-topped racing vehicles encouraged sleek leather outfits and helmets resembling early flying gear. Fashion was sometimes linked to motoring in unexpected ways, the first modern nail varnish or lacquer, developed c.1916, being originally inspired by automobile paint. Car ownership rose between the wars, although relatively few British households owned their own vehicles until after the Second World War. Mid-century driving clothes included leather driving gloves for gripping the wheel and short, hip-length car coats – 'sporty' clothes that reflected owners' pride in their vehicle and driving skills.

Golf

Played throughout Britain since the late-nineteenth century, golf has generally been regarded as a pursuit for the well-connected and financially comfortably placed. In areas where land is scarce – notably south-east England – historically golf-club membership has been restricted, yet in rural regions including much of Scotland (where the sport originated), Ireland and Wales, golfers have hailed from all walks of life. Golfing facilities multiplied rapidly around the turn of the century, the enthusiasm of Edward, Prince of Wales for the sport during the 1920s and 1930s enhancing its image further and golf-club membership becoming a desirable status symbol.

Before the First World War, male golfing clothes incorporating jacket and knee breeches were specially made by a man's tailor, female golfing dress generally a variant of existing country wear; woollen cloth jackets and skirts. From the 1910s onwards and, particularly, between the wars, men's and women's garments for the sport were regularly advertised in the press. A much-publicised innovation was the new golfing 'jacket', comfortable and loose-cut, allowing sufficient movement to freely swing a golf club.

Stretchy knitted garments were already worn for sports including cycling and rowing, and there developed a particularly close connection between golfing and knitwear, the newly fashionable cardigan even being referred to as a 'golfer'. The Prince of Wales personally favoured the Argyle pattern for his golfing sweaters, as displayed in Sir William Orpen's famous portrait of 1928 from the collection of the Royal and Ancient Golf Club of St Andrews. Another favourite was the Fair Isle sweater, featuring bands of coloured pattern on a neutral ground, worn on the golf course from the 1920s. With royal approval for vibrant knitwear, British men developed an uncharacteristic penchant for eye-catching golf clothes; along with wide tweed 'plus four' breeches, fancy coloured Argyle or checked socks, brogue shoes and flat cloth caps, this produced a distinctive golfing look, prompting much hilarity in novels and satirical *Punch* cartoons. Eventually from the late 1930s, wide 'plus fours' grew outmoded; more discreet flannel or worsted trousers were worn with plain jackets or sleeveless sweaters ('slip-overs') by mid-century male golfers.

Ladies' golf became increasingly fashionable between the wars, although many working- and lower-middle-class women were effectively

Snapshot photograph, early 1910s.

precluded from pursuing the sport by the time, travel and high costs involved; rather, female players were then typically middle-class and often older ladies. That said, female golf was on the rise; *Vogue* magazine featured the sport repeatedly during the 1920s and advertisements for beauty preparations used images of active young women playing golf to highlight the healthy properties of their products.

Because of the formal, rigid atmosphere at many golf clubs, and perhaps keen not to risk their place in a male-dominated arena, women avoided controversy and played safe on the golf course by wearing accepted 'sportswear' – a combination of comfortable sweaters, cardigans and skirts, with sturdy stockings and brogues. Clubs also had a tendency to set unnecessarily stringent regulations prohibiting certain female fashion details, such as decorative pleats on skirts or blouses with short sleeves. Trousers were completely unacceptable on the golf course during the 1920s and much of the 1930s, the old-fashioned, respectable costume of British players appearing stolid and un-stylish compared with the more modern, chic kit worn in tournaments by players from overseas.

Walking and Rambling

Unlike golf, walking for pleasure was first popularised by working people and remained a pursuit for 'every man'. During the early-nineteenth century, in response to the clamour, pollution and squalor of industrial towns and cities, a yearning for fresh air and more tranquil surroundings prompted mill and factory hands from northern manufacturing centres like Manchester, York, Leeds and Glasgow to step out into the nearby countryside. Associations aimed at securing convenient walking routes and preserving the landscape for human use were established as early as the 1820s, in recognition of city-dwellers' recreational needs. Indeed, early walking groups attracted members from quite diverse social and occupational backgrounds, all seeking escape from urban life in surrounding hills and dales.

Walking as a weekend activity became more common from the mid-1800s, aided greatly by the expanding Victorian railway network. Additionally, in the mid-1800s the Lancashire mill towns established Saturday as a half-day holiday for workers, the Bank Holiday Act of 1871 later giving others more leisure time in which to enjoy the countryside. Although the harshest, most remote regions remained inaccessible, for many of our mid- to late-Victorian ancestors, diverse areas of Britain came within easier reach, inspiring the formation of many organised walking and rambling groups. Initially, walking gear was based on existing tailored country clothes: male ramblers donned their tweed breeches, 'breathable' socks and cloth caps or straw hats before setting off into the countryside; women adopted masculine felt hats or shady straw boaters, stout boots and raised ankle-length hemlines, an important addition begin a sturdy umbrella that served as both walking stick and parasol.

During the early 1900s, railways carried growing numbers of walking enthusiasts deeper into the countryside, and after the First World War rambling in Britain progressed, becoming a nationwide movement. Walkers had always faced opposition from landowners and local authorities concerning use of land, and a major clash in 1932 known as the Mass Trespass of Kinder Scout moorland on what is now the Pennine Way, was a pivotal event in the battle over access to traditional footpaths. Further developments favouring walkers' rights of way coincided with a growing interest in the outdoors among people from all social backgrounds, fuelled by a new cult of health and fitness, fresh air and physical exercise.

Walking group photo from country house album, mid-1860s.

Walking was becoming more widely recognised as a means of building strength and stamina and encouraging a slender, athletic form – the new physical ideal. Gaining a suntan was also growing fashionable, and more relaxed leisure wear was designed to free and expose the limbs. While traditional tailored jackets, shirts and ties worn with breeches and sporting plus-fours were popular with older walkers between the wars, by the mid-1930s younger hikers and ramblers were adopting more modern outdoor wear, like that worn for cycling: shorts teamed with open-necked short-sleeved shirts, comfortable jerseys or light linen jackets. The colour of the new comfortable, practical separates was often khaki – the accepted colour for country camouflage; *en masse* it had a standardised appearance, which did not always meet with approval. For example, the artist William Russell Flint wrote to *The Times* in 1934 complaining of 'the spectacle of the country's youths and maidens invading the British countryside each weekend in hideous uniforms'. He wondered: 'Is hiking so stern a business that only the ugliest shades of wartime habiliments are considered appropriate?'

Conservative observers may well have been startled by the 'unisex' appearance of the shorts, loose linen jackets and sports' shirts worn by many of our parents and grandparents for open-air recreations in the 1930s and 1940s. Undoubtedly, walking clothes expressed the democratic character of the pursuit – instigated by ordinary working people and continuously enjoyed across the social spectrum. For wearers, the relaxed near-uniformity of modern outdoor clothes that blended with the landscape represented relief from competitive fashionable display or dreary conformity to sensible workwear. They were comfortable, fun and added to the sense of adventure, once everyday routine was left behind.

Postcard photograph of walking group, dated July 1938.

Chapter 7

Special Occasions

Historically the social elite typically changed their dress several times a day, wearing different fashionable outfits suited to hour and the occasion. Only our wealthier ancestors would have needed dedicated morning, afternoon and evening wear, appropriate for receiving friends at home, paying social calls, going out for lunch or tea, to formal afternoon functions, visiting the opera or theatre and attending soirées and balls. However, two important occasions – pivotal points in the human life cycle – were expressed through dress by rich and poor: marriage and death.

Bridalwear

Throughout history every female has wanted to look her best on her wedding day, although prior to the twentieth century most marriages were relatively low-key affairs. When tying the knot, our ordinary forebears and their friends and families wore their Sunday outfits – new or best-day clothes that could be used again in the future. Hosting an ostentatious 'white wedding' with bride decked out in special white attire suitable for only the one occasion was initially an elite practice, expanding during the later 1800s but uncommon before the early-twentieth century. Here we examine more closely the wedding dresses, bridegroom suits and bridal party trends that evolved between 1800 and 1950.

White garments – or ivory/off-white, as the colour originally appeared – were traditionally favoured for very formal attire, signifying prosperity and elevated social status. Fine white dress materials, expensive to buy and near-impossible to keep in good condition, were totally impractical for working people and therefore historically the preserve of a privileged minority. Thus, following sartorial precedent, by 1800 a luxurious white ensemble was the choice of high-ranking brides, the Christian associations of white with innocence and purity adding a spiritual symbolism to the worldly effect.

Fashion plate from *The Lady's Companion*, mid- to late 1850s.

Bridalwear followed the prevailing fashion and ethereal white muslin, net or gauze expressed perfectly the draped neo-classical modes of the early 1800s and 1810s; indeed, a white high-waisted gown featured in the earliest known British fashion plate depicting bridalwear, dating to June 1816. During the later 1820s and early 1830s, further bridal illustrations in upper- and middle-class publications showcased picturesque white silk satin or silk crepe pelisse gowns in the prevailing hourglass style, with full gigot sleeves and wide white collar, lace or embroidered veil cascading from a high chignon. While picturesque white bridalwear was gaining favour in high society, other fresh, youthful colours were also admired for young brides: shades such as cream/fawn, soft pink and pale blue were common, a clear sky blue especially popular with the rising middle classes.

By the mid- to late 1830s, a dainty white full-skirted gown was becoming the upper-class standard, accessorised with neat white gloves and ornate lace-edged veil or fashionable white bonnet. The event that transformed this vogue into an enduring tradition was the marriage of Queen Victoria to Prince Albert of Saxe-Coburg and Gotha in February 1840. Purposely departing from the heavy, regal state robes worn by former royal brides, the young queen chose a light, youthful *toilette* resembling the airiest of ball gowns. A creamy-white Spitalfields silk satin dress with deep flounce of Honiton lace and white satin court train ornamented with orange-blossom sprays was complemented by an orange-blossom wreath and Honiton lace veil. Victoria's twelve aristocratic train-bearers also wore white dresses and the charming impression created by the gathering of delicate white-clad ladies was skilfully captured in George Hayter's oil painting (1840–42), later circulated to a wide public via engraved prints and other souvenirs.

With royal approval for a romantic white bridal dress, veil and orange-blossom, the ladies' magazines that escalated from the mid-1800s onwards promoted and exaggerated the image, publishing idealised illustrations of demure brides in frothy white dresses and gossamer veils. All the trappings of the 'white wedding' known today also began to converge around this time: many local churches were modernised to provide superior settings for marriage ceremonies; bridal flowers became more fashionable, including orange-blossom, myrtle, lily of the valley, stephanotis, rosebuds, jasmine leaves and asparagus fern; decorative tiered wedding cakes of white sugar paste came into vogue; and elaborate table settings festooned with flowers and greenery were arranged for the wedding breakfast.

While the formal, costly 'white wedding' tradition was becoming established among wealthy families, such lavish events remained but a dream for many early-Victorian bridal couples. For brides from working backgrounds and lower-middle-class families, more practical was their existing Sunday outfit, or a new coloured day dress that could be reworn. Pale blue gowns remained fashionable, in plain or 'changeable' (shot) silk for those who could afford fine fabric, a sweeping or plunging V-neckline and rigid, pointed bodice dominating the 1840s. A simpler choice, common for summer and for country weddings, was a lighter frock of printed cotton fabric, woven with stripes, flowers or small abstract designs. Men also wanted to appear smart on their wedding day and many early-Victorian bridegrooms wore a formal frock coat, trousers, waistcoat, white shirt and good neckwear. With ornate waistcoats still in vogue, a prospective bridegroom sometimes ordered a special wedding waistcoat in white/cream silk or satin, embroidered or woven with lilies of the valley, acorns or other sentimental motifs. Alternatively, in the countryside a groom might well wear his Sunday smock-frock – a higher quality, more decorative garment than his everyday work smock.

Due to the rapid advance of commercial photography during the late 1850s and 1860s, from the mid-Victorian era onwards more photographic evidence survives for weddings and marriage attire. Most nineteenth-century wedding photographs were indoor studio portraits depicting the couple in fashionable day clothes, as worn earlier for the ceremony. Surviving wedding costumes add to the visual record, revealing that during the 1860s crinoline-style marriage gowns were often fashioned from silk material in vibrant aniline (synthetic) colours such as purple, magenta, azure blue and emerald green. Working- or middle-class grooms generally wore a smart morning coat, the more formal frock coat usual in high society.

The late 1860s also saw the emergence of open-air wedding photography for the few who could afford to commission a photographer to attend the occasion with all his complex apparatus. Luxurious group photographs composed in the spacious grounds of a villa or country house depict the ideal 'white wedding' of the age. Bride and attendants were adorned in clouds of white silk or tulle, their heads crowned with orange-blossom wreaths and lace or tulle veils, gentlemen wearing stately dark frock coats with contrasting trousers and tall top hats. Elite weddings of this nature also tended to be reported in local newspapers, providing useful and fascinating first-hand accounts of forebears whose celebrations were of interest to the wider community. For example, ancestors of family historian Simon Martin married at Hawkhurst in Kent in 1869, a detailed description of the festivities in the local press highlighting the 'picturesque and fine effect' of the 'rich dresses of the bridal party and the varied costumes of the visitors'. The bride, Miss Annie Gow-Steuart of Fowler's Park, Hawkhurst, '…was richly attired in white *poult de soie*, Brussels lace flounce and veil, wreath of orange blossoms and myrtle. There were eight bridesmaids … attired in white tarlatan, trimmed with pink satin, tulle veils and wreaths of pink moss rose buds.'

Bridal gowns – both luxurious ivory/white ensembles, as described above, and the good coloured daywear worn by most brides – continued to follow the fashionable line. In the later 1860s, skirts developed a pronounced backward sweep and from c.1869 overdresses were looped up into bouffant drapery over the protruding bustle (*tournure*) that would define bridal fashion until the mid-1870s (see coloured image no.7).

Family wedding photograph, Hawkhurst, Kent, dated 1869.

Afterwards, shaped by the new cuirass line, wedding gowns narrowed, the slender Princess dress popular both in bridal white and fashionable shades. During the 1870s, fashionable gowns were often generously trained, but when trains disappeared from regular daywear c.1880, a separate train attached at the waist or shoulders was retained for wedding gowns, for greater elegance during the bridal procession. Mid-Victorian brides choosing a special white gown were generally veiled, but most wore coloured daywear with a contemporary hat. Bridesmaids at formal white weddings no longer wore veils, but fashionable headwear, with identical pastel outfits complementing the bride's ensemble.

More wedding dress heirlooms survive from the later nineteenth century onwards, revealing the popular colours for bridal silks and velvets during the 1870s and 1880s, typically deep russets, claret, rich browns and dark greens, while brides mourning a deceased relative at the time of their marriage wore black, or muted mauve or grey tones representing half-mourning. During the early 1880s, all wedding dresses expressed the prevailing sheath-like silhouette; then, following fashion, the waistline rose c.1883/84 and bridal skirts developed the new bustle projection. In 1886 a major change occurred in canonical hours; previously marriage services had been conducted before noon, but could now be held after midday. This impacted on dress, for traditionally morning clothes were plainer than afternoon wear, the later church wedding ceremony prompting some brides to wear more formal afternoon costumes suitable for tea, dinner, or a handsome going-away outfit.

By the late 1800s, as aspirations grew and living standards improved among the fully employed, there was a growing tendency to incorporate elements of the exclusive 'white wedding' into regular family marriage celebrations. Late-Victorian wedding photographs suggest that brides from various backgrounds were now choosing hybrid costumes combining fine veil or fashionable white hat with a coloured daytime dress, their garments embellished with white accessories – a bodice sash or waist girdle and picturesque flower posy or corsage.

While economical studio wedding photography remained common, outdoor photography was also advancing, depicting extended bridal parties, including attendants and guests – larger group scenes that, along with exuberant 1890s' fashions, lent an air of grandeur to many contemporary weddings. Middle-class brides sometimes favoured special white gowns and veils, but with bold-coloured silk and satin fabrics, lace, frills, wide *gigot* sleeves and decorated plate-like hats fashionable for formal day wear, even relatively modest weddings conveyed an elaborate effect. Grooms, groomsmen and male wedding guests of the late-nineteenth century also appeared debonair in formal white neckties, gloves and *boutonnières*, a bowler hat worn with the popular lounge suit, silk top hat with the smarter morning and frock coats. There was tremendous variety in bridalwear at the end of Victoria's reign, but soon the full 'white wedding' would become more widely established.

Large group and open-air wedding photography became increasingly common during the early-twentieth century. Alongside traditional indoor studio portraits of newly-weds, more ambitious marriage scenes portrayed bride, groom and extended bridal party grouped wherever there was outdoor space. Even a modest wedding pictured in the family garden or farmyard appeared impressive: this must have elevated the occasion of marriage at this time, shaping how it would be viewed and remembered in the future. By the Edwardian era, fashion had abandoned the strident colours, heavy silks and stiff frills of the 1890s, favouring soft pastel shades and light, flowing fabrics such as chiffon and lace. As in earlier decades, and as would remain the case in future, mature brides who considered themselves too old for youthful white wedding apparel

Cabinet photograph, late 1890s.

chose discreet tones like mauve, grey or soft green. Poorer families continued to keep matters simple, favouring versatile clothes that could be reworn, yet the growing trend was for a special white wedding dress and veil, floral bouquet, bridesmaids and flower girls: the works.

Everything changed during the First World War and its aftermath, although initially brides were urged to put on a good show, to boost morale. Reports of society weddings and advertisements for luxury bridalwear tell of ivory or oyster satin, cream georgette, shimmering silver-grey velvet, shell-pink chiffon, gold lace and silver net – shining bridal materials that would complement a groom in smart military uniform. Ordinary brides wore an elegant off-white or soft-coloured gown fashioned in the prevailing narrow layered or asymmetrical tunic style, accessorised with stylish hat, or heirloom veil, fulfilling part of the requirement for 'something old, something new, something borrowed and something blue'.

As the conflict escalated, with marriages often organised at short notice to accommodate the groom's departure or brief leave, brides were rarely able to spend months planning their wedding or assembling a complex outfit. By 1915, when skirts became fuller and shorter, a picturesque calf-length white afternoon dress or belted suit and hat teamed with white stockings and dainty white shoes was fashionable for summer weddings.

Otherwise the smart suit or coat frock tailored in one of the characteristic blue, grey or brown wartime shades could be accessorised with stylish headwear and leather gloves.

Civilian life became re-established from 1919 and two royal weddings attracted public attention during the early 1920s: the marriage of King George V and Queen Mary's daughter, Princess Mary, to Viscount Lascelles in 1922, and that of their second son, Prince Albert, Duke of York, to Lady Elizabeth Bowes-Lyon in 1923. These opulent occasions and the fairy-tale royal bridal gowns of ivory and silver inspired a new generation, reviving the sense of romance that had been absent from wartime and early post-war weddings. Many 1920s' brides chose cream/ivory or a pastel colour such as soft blue, lilac, blush-pink or peach. Finer dresses were fashioned from silk and chiffon embellished with embroidery, lace, pearls and beads, net veils worn with headdresses worn low over the forehead. A knee-length coloured frock or suit was also fashionable as modern modes took hold during the mid- to late 1920s, the iconic fitted cloche hat and bar shoes completing the contemporary flapper look.

By the 1930s, many brides throughout society aimed for the popular 'white wedding', although there were exceptions; one strand of fashion favoured picturesque garden party dresses in floating flower-print georgette, chiffon or rayon, accessorised with a short 'coatee' jacket and wide-brimmed picture hat. More formal white wedding gowns attained a streamlined glamour under the influence of Hollywood films, graceful calf-length or longer trained dresses of silk or satin skilfully bias-cut to achieve a clinging drape. The medieval style, inspired by historical epic movies, found expression in slender gowns featuring elongated sleeves and round 'Juliet' caps suspending a trailing veil. By the late 1930s, long trained gowns in a cold, true white satin were replacing the soft ivories, creams and off-whites of the past. Sometimes woven in a damask-like flower pattern known as 'bridal satin', such wedding dresses were unequivocally special attire, unsuitable for any other occasion.

Weddings of the 1940s were dominated by the Second World War. Initially, formal 'white weddings' continued; despite (or because of) the privations of war and growing uniformity of civilian clothes, brides wanted their wedding day to be special, a dazzling occasion to recall during worsening times. But improvisation and ingenuity were required if bridal traditions were to continue. Elegant trained dresses from the late 1930s might be loaned by friends or relatives, some brides resurrecting their mothers' ivory wedding gowns from the 1910s and 1920s and altering them personally or using a professional dressmaker. If any material was left over it could then be utilised in the making of a hat or headdress.

New wedding gowns were sometimes available to buy during the war, although this was difficult for many with rationing; consequently, families often pooled precious coupons to purchase a special dress. Ready-made bridalwear was priced from around £4 upwards and might well cost over £20. Synthetic materials were cheaper than natural silk; for example, in 1944 Derry & Toms advertised a rayon satin bridal dress for £13 15s 6d and seven clothing coupons. However, in some parts of the country a waiting list of several months existed for new dresses, so many wartime brides resorted to making outfits at home. Curtain lace (exempt from the rationing points system) was often used to fashion a veil and long dress that could be worn over a white nightdress. Occasionally parachute silk was illegally acquired for making into wedding dresses or bridal lingerie for the trousseau.

Whatever fabric was used for the gown, there was generally little material to work with; consequently, the bodice was close-fitting, the skirt slender, without a traditional bridal train. Shallow V-shaped, square and heart-shaped sweetheart necklines were all in vogue and narrow sleeves using minimal fabric were puffed or padded at the shoulder. If material allowed, the bodice might be ruched, but generally new bridal gowns were simply styled, expressing an economical elegance. The bridal veil, attached to a late 1930s' tiara-style headdress or tall frame, was generally worn far back on the head, revealing carefully waved hair. Additional touches like gloves crocheted from white cotton helped to complete the bridal image, along with a modest bouquet and boot, heart or horseshoe suspended on ribbon – good luck tokens popular during the 1940s. Bridesmaids wore whatever matching or complementary clothing was available, dresses often of plain pastel-coloured or floral-printed material and adult bridesmaids wearing short shoulder-length veils.

As wartime shortages grew acute and the mood of austerity deepened, it seemed inappropriate to host an ostentatious 'white wedding'. In any event, most requisites for a conventional marriage were scarce or prohibited, from rice or confetti, to royal icing for the cake. Even wedding rings were elusive, due to the lack of gold for jewellery. Some women joined the waiting list for 9-carat utility wedding rings that famously turned the finger green; however, even those were in short supply and frequently an inherited ring was worn, or gold band borrowed for the ceremony. As early as June 1940 *Harper's Bazaar* had published a wedding feature promoting attractive suits and dresses in lieu of white bridalwear, and as the war advanced growing numbers of civilian brides married in smart daywear. Doubtless some of our female forebears felt disappointed at missing out on a dreamy white wedding, but others may have embraced the liberating sense of modernity as they walked confidently down the aisle in chic utility outfit and stylish accessories. A fitted knee-length dress or sharp tailored suit, jaunty hat tilted over a glamorous

My Aunt and Uncle's wedding photograph, dated November 1944.

hairstyle and floral corsage pinned to the lapel or neat bouquet held in a gloved hand typified the civilian bridal wartime look.

During the war, bridegrooms serving with the armed forces customarily wore military uniform on their wedding day. As the war progressed, many more females joined military units and support organisations, often becoming betrothed to fellow servicemen. British women in the forces received no coupons for civilian dress, so special bridalwear was usually unattainable and they too might marry in uniform. Immediately after the war, the popularity of weddings peaked. Until demobilised or during national service, bridegrooms continued to wear service uniform. Otherwise the average groom wore his demob suit, a pre-war civilian lounge suit or, if fortunate, a new suit tailored in the wide pre-war style. Middle- and upper-class grooms revived the tradition of hiring a formal morning suit: dark tail coat, grey striped trousers, top hat, a silk cravat and white gloves. With clothes rationing still in place, many post-war bridal dresses purchased or made in Britain retained their slender appearance, although modest trains reappeared and wedding outfits of the late 1940s increasingly reflected the New Look style. Some brides were thrilled to be presented in 1945 or 1946 with beautiful white dresses or fine materials from overseas, including wedding gowns from high-end New York department stores, or lengths of Italian silk or lace, by grooms who had served abroad.

The marriage of Princess Elizabeth to Prince Philip Mountbatten in November 1947 was a glorious event that symbolised the ending of the bleak war years. The princess' wedding gown, designed by Norman Hartnell, was fashioned from ivory silk satin from the Scottish firm Winterthur and encrusted with American seed pearls, the 15-yard-long satin train being woven at Lullingstone in Kent. The dress bodice featured a fashionable sweetheart neckline and the long tulle veil was attached to a diamond fringe tiara, the whole ensemble achieving a perfect balance of femininity and glamour. Like all new wedding dresses, the royal gown required coupons and reportedly hundreds of brides-to-be throughout the country offered their clothing coupons to the princess. Yet, despite the fairy-tale wedding, Britain remained in the grip of economic recession and economical utility-style outfits remained a common choice throughout the late 1940s and beyond.

Mourning Attire

Many of us are intrigued by the seemingly morbid mourning rituals adopted by earlier generations following the passing of a loved one or an important public figure – customs far removed from most practices today. The notion of wearing sombre black apparel symbolising death and melancholy, for months if not years, does not accord closely with modern sensibilities, yet to examine this complex aspect of dress is to understand more about our ancestors' worlds.

In 1800, the tradition of adopting special mourning attire following the death of a relative, close friend or royalty was already well established within the upper echelons of society. The public wearing of heavy black or drab clothing and accoutrements expressed the personal grief of the bereaved and also demonstrated their correct observance of social custom. With mourning dress largely following prevailing styles in garments, accessories and jewellery, it was also firmly linked to high fashion – at one level another occasion for sartorial display. The wearing of mourning clothes was also filtering down through society, growing common among the middle and lower classes.

The novelist Jane Austen hailed from a large, genteel family and often had to don mourning apparel, remarks in her personal correspondence indicating the considerable expense involved in acquiring the correct clothes for such occasions. With few dress articles then available to buy ready-made, new gowns and other fitted garments had to be fashioned from scratch. Assembling a full mourning costume could be problematic if a death occurred suddenly, or if dress budgets were limited. Indeed, Jane and her relatives often improvised, dyeing existing clothes black and covering ordinary caps and bonnets with dull black mourning fabrics. Other sources confirm that dyeing clothes black at home, or sending silk items out to be dyed by a professional silk dyer, was common throughout society; it might then only be necessary to purchase new black trimmings for a gown.

In 1814, when London society mourned the death of Queen Charlotte's brother, the Duke of Mecklenburg-Strelitz, Jane Austen wore a brown gown to an evening function. While black was ideal for deep mourning, brown and, especially, lilac and grey, as well as white, were all recognised mourning shades. Evidently there was flexibility in such matters in the early 1800s and in all probability less well-off urban and rural families wore their usual Sunday outfits (often of dark or sombre colours, anyway) to funerals. As for the very poor, reserving items exclusively for special mourning occasions would have been an impossible luxury.

As the nineteenth century advanced, mourning rituals became more widespread and increasingly elaborate, interest in mourning dress growing more pronounced during Queen Victoria's reign. Undoubtedly, the British public were influenced by the visible symbols of the monarch's personal loss and self-imposed eternal mourning following the untimely death of Prince Albert in 1861. However, the Victorian 'cult' of mourning, already entrenched, was also a product of industry – manufacturing progress and escalating commercialism. The first mourning warehouse in London, Jay's, opened on Regent Street in 1841 – an emporium selling every conceivable item expressing bereavement and loss; this was followed by more dedicated shops, large outfitters and mourning departments of stores offering a growing array of mourning fabrics, accessories and jewellery – important items in our predecessors' wardrobes.

Mourning was also an intricate social ritual. As outlined in Chapter 2, domestic manuals and etiquette books proliferated from the mid-1800s, aimed at guiding the *nouveaux riches* and others unsure of social protocol through the maze of Victorian manners and mores. These authoritative publications, and middle-class fashion periodicals, set out detailed mourning specifications, 'rules' that grew ever more labyrinthine, the mourning periods longer, as time went by. Victorian and Edwardian mourning was highly complex and Lou Taylor examines the topic in detail in her seminal work, *Mourning Dress*. By way of brief summary here, the nature and length of recommended mourning depended on the relationship of the bereaved to the deceased; so, for instance, the death of a parent, child or sibling usually prompted the wearing of 'deeper' (stricter) mourning attire and for longer than the passing of a distant cousin. Friends and close associates – neighbours and work colleagues – were also mourned to varying degrees, as might be members of the royal family and other public figures.

Family mourning photograph dated September 1898

By any standards, women bore the heaviest burden, particularly widows, who were urged to publicly mourn their husbands for at least 2½ years. At the height of the fashion for mourning dress, between approximately 1850 and 1890, a widow was expected to progress through the predetermined stages of 'deep' or 'First' mourning (wearing sombre, monochrome black for at least one year and a day), followed by 'Second' mourning for a further nine months, towards the end of which she was theoretically permitted some jet trimmings; after the first twenty-one months she could enter 'Third' or 'Ordinary' mourning, adding small amounts of silk and lace; and when two years had passed following her loss, she could enter the 'Half-mourning' phase and progress to the half-mourning shades of grey, mauve and white. Logically, not everybody could, or would, have followed such dictates to the letter, while many older widows never donned colours again, adhering to sober black, or muted half-mourning colours for the rest of their lives.

Female mourning attire largely followed the style of fashionable dress and theoretically every dress article was deep black, until contrasting touches were acceptable during the later stages, as outlined above. Non-reflective textiles were recommended as, following long-held custom, nothing about mourning dress was supposed to shine or gleam, although photographic evidence in the form of mourning portraits paints a more varied picture. Apparently fashionable black silks and velvets were common in the 1850s and 1860s, but largely gave way by the 1870s to dull garments without a sheen, presumably representing plain, matt black materials developed especially for Victorian mourning. These were numerous, and multiplied over time, common types including bombazine/bombasin (worsted/silk material); barathea (ditto) and paramatta (a cheaper cloth of worsted and cotton).

The textile most closely associated with mourning was black crêpe (or crape, a mourning term) – crimped, dull gauze fabric with a distinctive textured appearance. Crape could be used to cover the entire skirt of a gown for First or deep mourning, but might be limited to bodice panels, cuffs and skirt trimmings. Mourning specifications also included special accessories such as bags and gloves and personal ornaments, so sombre jewellery of costly black jet or cheaper black glass ('French jet') replaced shining gold brooches, pendants and bracelets; even dress chains and watch chains were made of dull, dark metal. More economical still, for poorer mourners, was the mourning jewellery made of humble materials like Irish bog oak.

For some of our ancestors, including the working classes, an important element of the ritual involved being formally photographed wearing requisite black mourning attire – solemn portraits representing bereavement and personal loss, while also recording fulfilment of social expectations. Old mourning photographs in today's family collections portray groups or individuals – rarely men alone, but often women, chiefly widows. Widows' mourning headwear was very diverse, its form reflecting the fashions of the day and the wearer's

CROWE & RODGERS   STIRLING.

Mourning cdv dated 1883.

age, personal taste, social and financial situation. Widows' headdresses included modest black bonnets, ornate black caps featuring long crape streamers ('falls') and dramatic veiled hats. Half-mourning white crape caps with falls, like those worn by Queen Victoria, were also popular from the later 1800s, available to buy boxed, in sets.

Apart from Victorian undertakers and chief mourners in traditional black cloaks, sashes and trailing crape hat 'weepers', male mourning dress was far less conspicuous than women's attire. Sometimes a widower ordered a new black mourning waistcoat to go with a regular black suit and necktie; an optional black armband or hatband might also be worn, yet photographic evidence is surprisingly scant. By the last quarter of the nineteenth century, small children generally only wore mourning clothes following the loss of a parent or sibling. Sylvia's *How to Dress Well on a Shilling a Day* (1875) stated: 'It is desirable that children should be put into mourning dress as seldom as possible; only in fact for the nearest relatives. The little children do not understand it and it is absurd to invest them with the signs of grief they cannot feel.'

Children of 4 or 5 and upwards were dressed in black or dark clothes with white accessories, babies' and toddlers' white garments trimmed with black/dark ribbons. It was changing attitudes concerning children that pioneered the gradual decline of mourning dress.

By the 1890s, Victorian sensibilities no longer favoured the oppressive mourning rituals of previous decades. Dress codes were becoming less rigidly applied, this trend reflected in an apparent sharp decrease in formal mourning photographs by 1900. The nation adopted 'general mourning' briefly, following the deaths of Queen Victoria in January 1901 and King Edward VII in May 1910, but this was the swansong of the ritual that had so preoccupied earlier generations. The terrible loss of life during the First World War further eroded the meaning of mourning, changing the context of mourning dress; some reported that the streets were 'full of black-clad women', but many simply wore a black armband, also permitted for those in uniform. The wartime government even actively encouraged people not to spend their precious resources on black mourning apparel, for fear it would damage the regular domestic garment and textile industries at a precarious time.

Mourning dress continued to decline after the war, especially among the middling classes who usually pioneered the most progressive ideas. In general, extended public mourning persisted for longer among the conservative upper classes, and conversely within poorer communities;

also in deeply religious families from all social backgrounds. It is interesting to speculate whether – and to what extent – earlier generations of our own families followed recommended mourning practices, but difficult to know for sure, unless surviving photographs, explicit documents or reliable oral accounts offer clues. Many researchers assume that extended public mourning in prescribed apparel was mainly an upper- and middle-class tradition; and yet, while prosperous ancestors could afford more elaborate mourning, burying the dead decently and showing respect by wearing the correct clothes was equally important – if not more so – among poorer and working-class families. Social commentators including Charles Dickens openly condemned the way in which the demands of mourning encouraged ostentation and excessive expenditure among the wealthy, while putting undue pressure on the poor who could ill-afford the expense, yet often found ways and means.

Evening Dress

Marriage and death each prompted the wearing of special clothes to mark a single or occasional key event. Evening wear has been another recognised form of dress that meant little to most of our forebears in 1800, but that, as living standards rose for many and new forms of entertainment emerged, were a familiar element in the wardrobe a century later.

For affluent, well-connected nineteenth-century ancestors there were many opportunities for display of luxurious garments at evening functions, and over the decades, as sartorial etiquette grew more intricate, different degrees of evening *toilette* evolved. By the late-Victorian period a lady might have to consider such ensembles as dinner dress, reception dress, home dinner toilette, evening demi-toilette, concert toilette, evening dress and ball dress. These diverse terms implied differing levels of formality according to the importance of the occasion; in practice, this meant variations in neckline, sleeve length, weight of fabric and amount of ornamentation.

Female evening fashions of the 1800s followed the lines of regular day dress, but featured a lower décolletage and shorter sleeves, while using more costly materials and fragile trimmings. Accessory-wise, white kid gloves, exquisite fans and delicate floral, feathered or jewelled hair ornaments were much in vogue (see coloured image No.8); indeed, for high-ranking ladies, formal attendance at court required obligatory trained gowns, long gloves, fan and plumed headdress. In general, lighter, airier and flimsier gowns were worn for balls, since poorly ventilated ballrooms crammed with dancers soon became unbearably hot. Conversely, dinners, concerts and more intimate parties might suggest a more elegant or handsome ensemble with longer sleeves. Young, unmarried females just entering 'society' were encouraged to wear white or pastel-coloured evening wear in muslin, tulle, net and other diaphanous materials, set off by youthful pearl ornaments, while sumptuous, richly coloured gowns and heavy, glittering gemstones were deemed more appropriate for married ladies. As late as 1899, the *Illustrated London News* asserted:

Cabinet photograph, early 1890s.

'All that a girl wears should be gay and light-looking, the opposite of the touch of stateliness and the settled air that become her young matron sister.'

By the turn of the twentieth century, more of our ancestors had occasion to don special evening wear; many communities held public dances, while membership of sports and social clubs, educational organisations, business and charitable associations, all manner of groups could also entail participation in dinners, balls and formal gatherings. The growing trend towards acquisition of a separate outfit for evening wear is reflected in family photographs from the 1890s onwards, as is a growing interest in 'fancy dress' – picturesque costumes representing mythological characters, favourite figures from history or folklore, national dress and patriotic themes.

Edwardian evening wear evolved to follow the sinuous *Art Nouveau* aesthetic of the early 1900s. The curvaceous female silhouette was accentuated by shimmering evening gowns, the bodice featuring narrow shoulder straps and clinging skirt sweeping out towards a fish-tail hemline. Admired materials included silk, satin, chiffon, muslin and net, generously embellished with applied decoration: lace, embroidery, beads and sequins. Such an ensemble was completed with long fitted gloves, fan, pearl or diamond choker necklace, and, for the most prestigious events, a regal tiara – the most iconic jewellery item of the period.

While convention dictated the most traditional, graceful evening attire, modern popular culture also increasingly influenced twentieth-century dress, with new forms of commercial music and dancing ushering in more *avant garde* evening modes. Syncopated ragtime music from America arrived in Britain around 1911, introducing livelier dance steps, followed by the controversial tango c.1912, and finally jazz in around 1917. The performance of fashionable dances such as the 'Turkey Trot' and 'Grisly Bear' involving more movement were facilitated by softer, pliable dance and sports corsets incorporating flexible elastic panels in place of rigid boning. Evening wear at this time favoured slender gowns sashed below the bust, layered tunic gowns and daring harem pants pioneered by Parisian *couturier* Paul Poiret. Created from floating chiffons, sensuous silks and plush velvets in vibrant colours, evening fashions in the years around the First World War also owed much to the theatrical influence and imagined 'orientalism' of Léon Bakst and Sergei Diaghilev's acclaimed Ballets Russes.

The war changed society and afterwards a young, pleasure-seeking generation frequented the public dance halls, nightclubs and new jazz venues opening in towns and cities nationwide. New dances like the Charleston and foxtrot had to be learned and dance schools flourished, although the different strata of society still frequented separate establishments for their nights out. The upper and upper-middle classes tended to favour private clubs, exclusive hotels and restaurants, while the lower-middle and working classes enjoyed visiting large pay-to-enter commercial ballrooms like Hammersmith Palais and Birmingham's Palais de Dance, many learning to move skilfully around the dance floor.

Women's evening dresses of the early 1920s could be striking, yet remained essentially elegant, worn to low-calf or ankle-length in dramatic colours, and ornamented with appliqué work, tassels and beads. A new fashion was the *kokoshnik*-style tiara headdress, a Russian-inspired mode, often worn with sumptuous fur-trimmed evening cloak or coat, and accessorised with ostrich-feather fan. After mid-decade, as the craze for jazz music and energetic dancing advanced, bold new tubular, knee-length flapper dance frocks in dazzling white, jet black, jade green, lacquer red, deep rose, burnt orange, even metallic fabrics, were all the rage.

Layered, split skirts, tiers of swaying fringes, glittering glass beads and sequins, jewelled and diamanté trimmings, strings of eye-catching beads and long feather boas reflected the light and accentuated movement.

Bars, dancing and cocktail parties seem to epitomise fashionable 1930s' nightlife. At cheap public dances known as 'bob hops' dress regulations were relaxed, and simple cotton dance frocks could be worn. Yet, conversely, influenced by Hollywood films, luxurious evening wear also gained heightened allure. Graceful draped evening gowns featured lowered hemlines, ankle length or trailing languidly on the floor, while soft materials like gleaming satin and clinging crêpe de Chine in coral, powder blue, eau de nil, taupe or classic black were bias-cut, moulding fabric to figure. At the high end of fashion, scintillating dresses featured asymmetrical necklines worn off one shoulder, or dipped to a daringly low V at the back, revealing golden, newly bronzed flesh. Accessories of the decade included gold and silver lamé dance shoes, velvet evening coats, deep fur stoles and shoulder capes. Glistening waved hair framed glowing faces highlighted with movie-star cosmetics: bright lipstick, rouged cheeks, mascara, glossed eyelids and arched plucked eyebrows. Bold 1930s' evening styles expressed a more modern, overtly sexual type of glamour, but experienced a sudden hiatus during the Second World War.

Men's evening attire was also important, becoming more widely worn, like women's evening dress, later in our period. During the early 1800s, coloured tail or 'dress' coats were worn with fitted white or pale-coloured breeches or pantaloons, white stockings and black buckled leather shoes. When daywear began to grow more sober and standardised, black became *de rigeur* for the evening dress or tail coat, tailored from fine milled cloth and usually featuring silk or velvet collar and facings. This was teamed with fitted knee breeches, black silk stockings and soft dress

Evening wear, from H.J. Nicholl & Co. catalogue, c.1929.

shoes. The white evening dress shirt featured a decorative pleated or frilled front; initially the waistcoat – often the focus of attention – could be coloured, but after mid-century was usually black or white. A white waistcoat was correct for full evening dress, with a white necktie, a formal outfit completed with white evening gloves and a collapsible opera hat (top hat with a spring in the crown) or *gibus*.

Reflecting changing daytime fashions but lagging somewhat behind, after the mid-1800s, the black dress or tail coat was partnered with close-fitting black dress trousers. For 'full' evening dress, reserved for the most important functions, a stiffly starched white evening shirt with winged collar was considered correct, along with white waistcoat, silk opera hat, white gloves, cane and evening cloak or coat. This seemingly 'timeless' style continued into the twentieth century, its popularity ensured by the debonair evening dress worn on stage and screen, especially in musicals featuring Fred Astaire and English actor Jack Buchanan.

Simultaneously, from the 1880s an alternative, more relaxed evening suit also evolved, featuring a short evening lounge or dinner jacket (called the Tuxedo in America), tailored in cloth or velvet. During the twentieth century, the dinner jacket, worn with black bow tie, was popular for less formal evening events such as private dinner parties, the theatre and concerts. As with female evening fashions, male evening dress became more significant in many people's wardrobes after the First World War, in response to modern popular culture – the rise of cinema, new forms of music and love of dancing.

Chapter 8

Making and Buying

Learning to Sew

Historically, sewing was considered an essential feminine accomplishment. Before the machine age, girls from all walks of life learned to sew by hand from the age of 5 or 6, often being taught at home, alongside instruction in other household tasks. Some would ultimately be able to create entire garments and many would at least stitch their own linen caps, kerchiefs, aprons, shifts and

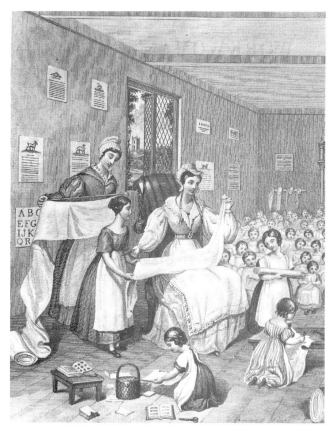

Frontispiece of
The Workwoman's Guide, 1838.

other underclothes, simple baby clothes, men's shirts and cravats. Sewing and ornamenting basic dress articles, including the family linen, was deemed a fundamental female duty in the nineteenth and early-twentieth centuries, to the extent that even after sons left home, until they married, their mothers and sisters often carried on making their shirts.

Although most girls (and some boys) gained sewing skills at home, from the early 1800s schools were also encouraged to include needlework in the curriculum and many Victorian dame schools, village schools, Sunday schools and orphanages taught sewing. As the education system expanded, domestic subjects became compulsory for girls to equip them for their future roles as wives and mothers, and to prepare them for possible jobs in domestic service, tailoring, dressmaking or millinery. Surviving school cloth 'account' or sampler books demonstrate the nature of their work, which included various needle crafts, from knitting, crochet and fine sewing, to plain stitching and creating the gussets and gores used in garment making.

Teachers were issued with practical instruction books like *Needlework and Cutting Out* (1884) by Kate Stanley, Head Governess and Teacher of Needlework at Whitelands College, Chelsea. In addition to the techniques exemplified in their school 'account' books, girls learned to hem, sew and fell seams, sew on buttons, attach tape strings, to gather and tuck fabric, and patch, darn and strengthen thinning material. Basics mastered, they then progressed to cutting-out and making-up, learning to fashion 'Baby's First Shirt; a Nightgown; a Long White Petticoat; a Robe and Pinafore for Baby; a Woman's Chemise (blouse) and Gored Flannel Petticoat.'

Home Work

During adulthood, needlecrafts or 'work' remained a customary pastime for privileged ladies – a genteel and useful occupation to turn to during long hours of leisure time. Many middle-and upper-class women created decorative furnishings for the home, small articles such as handkerchiefs, bags, mittens and slippers for themselves, and as gifts for relatives and friends. It was also customary to spend time sewing essentials for the poor: plain clothes, household linen, 'maternity boxes' for expectant mothers, even burial shrouds. Sewing for the needy was well-established by Jane Austen's day. In *Mansfield Park* Mrs Norris reminded Fanny: 'if you have no work of your own, I can supply you from the poor-basket.'

During the Victorian era, women's philanthropic institutions and sewing societies proliferated and grew highly organised, producing impressive quantities of clothes for the 'deserving poor'. Our more affluent female ancestors may well have been involved in such initiatives – or conversely, if poor, may have been recipients of charitable clothing gifts.

Otherwise, much women's sewing was geared towards domestic consumption. Whereas many men's ready-made items were becoming available by the mid-1800s, most female garments, being generally more varied in style and complex in construction, were made from scratch until mass-production advanced in the twentieth century. Assembling a lady's costume could be a slow process, for it meant purchasing and working with every individual requisite, from fabric and sewing thread to trimmings. Jane Austen and her associates sometimes altered or ornamented existing garments and enjoyed decorating hats, caps and bonnets; indeed, renovating and embellishing headwear at home, using fashionable ribbons, bows, lace, feathers and flowers, was still common

Fashion plate from *La Belle Assemblée*, June 1812.

in the early-twentieth century. Otherwise privileged ladies relied upon maid servants, or employed trusted garment-makers for help with major sewing projects.

Jane Austen and her sister, Cassandra, usually had their gowns and pelisses made by recognised dressmakers or 'mantua-makers' – the Georgian term for 'dressmaker', still used in the early to mid-1800s. Given a choice, women preferred to use the services of a skilled professional; an expertly made garment generally looked superior to the home-made equivalent. Experienced dressmakers and seamstresses, like male tailors, operated in cities, towns and villages nationwide, between them serving a wide population. Some were exclusive, high-end professionals, while others undertook affordable sewing for working-class clients unable or too busy to do their own domestic needlework; for example, some factory or mill hands working long shifts earned sufficient wages to employ others to do their sewing. In some cases it made financial sense to use outside dressmakers and seamstresses for certain tasks; however, for many ordinary women, personally making, altering and repairing at least some items for the family was a necessary economy in the nineteenth and early-twentieth centuries.

Paper Patterns and Sewing Machines

Successful home sewing depended on available resources and in the early 1800s home dressmaking could be time-consuming. Aprons, shifts, men's shirts and other loose or unshaped linen or cotton items were relatively easy to make, but fitted clothes like gowns, pelisses and jackets needed a reliable template to follow when cutting out the fabric. Home dressmakers often copied an existing garment, sometimes unpicking seams to create a flat 'model' which was traced on to thin paper or directly on to the lining material of the new garment. Friends and relatives also shared and circulated such patterns based on their favourite existing clothes.

During the Victorian era, advancing technology and an increase in printed material made a significant impact on the construction of clothes. As outlined in Chapter 2, by the mid-1800s growing numbers of instruction manuals and fashion-led periodicals were being produced, aimed mainly at the rising middle classes. Some, including *The Englishwomen's Domestic Magazine*, began to issue free small-scale paper garment patterns alongside their fashion illustrations – or readers were invited to apply for them by post. Early patterns for dress items like underwear, bodices and mantles were generally all printed on one large sheet of paper, the home dressmaker then tracing off the required parts and adjusting them for size.

In time, commercial pattern companies became established, America's Butterick and McCall's founded respectively in 1863 and 1870, Butterick operating in Britain by 1876. Their cut-out pattern pieces in white tissue paper had notches and perforations by way of directions: there were no printed markings as yet. Using such patterns, ideally the inexpensive cotton dress-lining was first cut out and fitted directly against the body; when a good fit was achieved then the lining pieces became the model or *toile* for cutting out the more costly garment material.

Rising demand for paper dressmaking patterns was fuelled by the development of the domestic sewing machine. The earliest working machine is usually said to be that patented by Thomas Saint in London, 1790, for sewing leather; however, it was American Elias Howe who patented the first practical lock-stitch sewing machine using the two threads familiar in domestic machines today. Isaac Singer followed in 1851 with an improved, more efficient model, the name of Singer becoming synonymous with the new equipment. In 1856, Singer launched a sewing-machine agency in Glasgow, his machines reaching British home dressmakers through retail shops. Other brands also emerged and by the late 1860s there existed around twenty different domestic sewing machines.

Many early sewing machines were expensive at around £10 to £15 – too costly for many independent home dressmakers. Some models were cheaper, however, and ultimately prices in general reduced by the 1890s, when sales surged. Sometimes friends, relatives and neighbours clubbed together, sharing a hand-crank or treadle machine, while some acquired machines using hire-purchase systems. Access to a

Cdv photograph, late 1860s.

sewing machine brought considerable advantages to the home dressmaker, enabling long seams and lengths of trimming to be stitched very quickly; yet, ironically, the speed of machine sewing probably encouraged the use of ever more stitching and highly complex trimmings: the art of dressmaking had become both simpler, and potentially more complicated.

Electricity provided a new form of power, beginning in the 1880s, when the first urban streets gained electricity supplies. Singer developed its first electric sewing machine in 1889, although many British homes were not connected to electricity until well after the creation of the national grid in 1926. During the later 1920s and 1930s, more households began to acquire electric sewing machines, while simultaneously clothing styles grew simpler, no longer requiring the traditional precision of fit. Fashionable garments from short children's clothes to shift-like tennis dresses were now becoming easier to make, inspiring a new generation of home dressmakers.

Pattern companies also became more competitive, making their patterns easier to use. In 1921, McCall pioneered printed patterns on large sheets of tissue with dart placements, notches for matching pieces and

Picturesque Dressing-Gowns

THE dressing-gowns of to-day are exceedingly picturesque. The correct one nowadays is the lovely straight robe which clings to the figure and which is quite dainty enough to be worn at the breakfast table. In this connection the kimono outline reigns supreme, and many of the prettiest bedroom gowns are of the pull-on order, confined at the waist by crossed ribbons or a tasselled girdle. Cashmere or nun's veiling makes an ideal déshabillé, or printed voile, the collar and cuffs turned back with satin or pongee.

WONDERFUL RESULTS.

Girls who embroider can easily achieve wonderful results with a length of soft cashmere, in a neutral tint, and some iron-off designs of Japanese persuasion. The designs are outlined with crewel silks, and —perhaps—some of the interstices are filled with black or white floss silk. Or, again, the pattern could be filled in with a flat wash of water-colour in which a little Chinese white has been mixed. This kind

of decoration is very popular in Paris and can be quite easily done at home. The important point to remember is that the material should be stretched—but not too tightly—and that the paint should not be at all thick. Gouache colours are very easily applied, and the best effects are obtained with a mixture of outline embroidery and flat washes.

THE BEST COLLAR.

For pull-on dressing-gowns a rather wide halter collar is best, and the sleeves should be of pagoda form and very loose at the wrist. A thoroughly useful déshabillé might be made of dark blue cashmere—or pongee—with embroidered motifs worked in dull rose and white silks strewn here and there quite carelessly. The halter collar and turn-back cuffs could be dull rose satin and the girdle a discreet mixture of dark blue, rose, and white. Black and white dressing-gowns, with a touch of bright colour somewhere, are always distinguished, and all the soft grey shades are attractive.

A paper pattern (No. 19), price 1s. post free, may be obtained of this becoming dressing-gown from "The Daily Mail" Paper Pattern Dept., 29 1a, Oxford-street, W. 1.

Paper pattern from the *Daily Mail*, 8 March 1921.

other useful devices including naming each separate piece, following this innovation in 1924 with more detailed directions. Eventually other companies did likewise, creating more user-friendly patterns with clear instructions – the prototype of modern garment patterns. Patterns were widely available by mail order, or from local shops, also being included as supplements in many women's home and fashion magazines. Dedicated weekly and monthly sewing and needlecraft periodicals also proliferated, guiding readers in everything from making dressing-gowns to embroidering evening bags.

Make-do and Mend

Women managing small domestic budgets were long accustomed to making new clothes and accessories, as well as mending and remodelling old garments to extend their useful life. During the First World War, with escalating inflation and many household incomes reduced, it became even more important to make economies in dress; women sewed affordable, functional garments for themselves and adapted existing items to clothe their children. When war broke out again in September 1939, British civilians entered an age of shortages and austerity, during which dress would be severely limited as never before. For the next decade or more, our mothers, grandmothers and great grandmothers had to use all the tricks in the book to keep their families decently clothed.

Almost immediately after war erupted, essential material goods began to grow scarce. During the conflict, some dress items disappeared completely and most new clothing purchases were strictly rationed from June 1941. The government aimed to reduce consumer demand so that all resources could be directed towards the war effort and in 1942 the Board of Trade launched a 'Make-do and Mend' campaign to encourage civilians to, 'utilise every old garment before considering anything new'. As Hugh Dalton, the Board's president, explained: 'When you are tired of your old clothes, remember that by making them do you are contributing some part of an aeroplane, a gun or a tank.' Picturesque cartoon character, 'Mrs Sew and Sew', personified the scheme on posters and the press played their part by circulating practical tips. Numerous 'how-to' publications advised on the care of clothing, while newspaper features like the 'Sew and Save' articles in the *Daily Mail* explained every step of home dressmaking and planning a smart, functional wartime wardrobe.

The concept of 'Make-do and Mend' appealed to the British public's keen sense of patriotism. Millions of ordinary women could already sew competently and were accustomed to making clothes last, but privileged ladies struggling without domestic help were less familiar with basic tasks. For the inexperienced, the Women's Voluntary Service and Women's

Institute ran Make-do and Mend evening classes, while some women taught themselves the fundamentals of home dressmaking. However, even with sewing skills, garment-making was undermined by fabric shortages and women had to improvise. Winter coats were fashioned from blankets, dresses created from blackout material or old curtains; some women transformed their absent husband's dressing-gowns and overcoats into coats and jackets for themselves. Parachute silk was occasionally used to make underwear and wedding dresses; worn adults' clothes were remade into children's garments. Resourceful dressmakers used any available scraps to create wearable, if unusual, garments including silk map-patterned blouses and dressing-gowns. Patriotic materials were also popular, like the red, white and blue 'Victory' print. Indeed, managing the wardrobe and domestic sewing proved crucial for maintaining morale and a sense of normality during the war: needle and thread became 'weapons' of ingenuity, determination and resilience.

Hand-Knitting

Knitting is a needlecraft involving the creation of fabric from a single thread formed into horizontal rows of loops that interlock with each subsequent row. Historically, in Britain, knitted clothing items using various yarns included caps, stockings/hose, gloves and underwear, with woollen yarn often favoured for its softness and warmth. Some areas like the Yorkshire Dales were early domestic and commercial knitting centres, the craft there spanning the late-sixteenth to early-twentieth centuries. From the late 1700s, 'knit-frocks' or knitted 'jackets' – what we would term sweaters or jerseys – were key dress items in many coastal areas, the comfortable, hard-wearing blue or grey knitted Guernsey sweater or 'gansey' becoming a staple of the seafaring man's wardrobe. Knitting these special articles from four- or five-ply worsted wool, for family and local wear (and sometimes for sale) typically involved whole communities, who often developed their own unique knitted designs.

More generally, in the early 1800s knitting was a genteel craft associated particularly with mature ladies and invalids, although it was also taught as a useful skill in orphanages and poor houses. It became more fashionable with the development of fine steel knitting needles and was increasingly taught in schools, along with other practical needle crafts. Fine Victorian items included lace-like knitted shawls, collars, cuffs and baby gowns, as well as decorative knitted and beaded items for the home. Sturdy knitted sweaters, stretchy and comfortable, began to be worn by sportsmen including oarsmen and cyclists, and were also the common dress of children in poor communities. From the early 1900s, knitted sweaters and women's cardigans were increasingly adopted for leisure activities like walking, skiing, golf and tennis. During the First World War, many women hand-knitted cosy 'comforts' for the troops: socks, gloves, mufflers, body-warmers, jerseys and balaclavas. Equally, knitting was an economical way of extending the family's wardrobe during the war; many women produced infants' garments and relaxed knitted caps and belted cardigan-style jackets for themselves.

Cdv photograph, mid-1870s.

During the 1920s and 1930s, hand-knitted garments entered everyday dress for all. Commercial knitting patterns were manufactured in large quantities by companies such as Weldon's, Leach's and Jaeger, who also produced their own magazines with instructions for knitting everything from underclothes and baby outfits to schoolboys' sweaters, men's slip-over vests and sets of matching winter hats, mufflers and gloves. Women's fashion and home magazines also included knitwear patterns for plain and more decorative garments. Argyle and Fair Isle designs were especially popular, the introduction of novelty yarns like angora and mohair giving knitting a further boost.

After war erupted again in 1939, hand-knitting became essential to the home front concept of 'remaking and making-do', the Women's Voluntary Services leading a nationwide knitting drive. When most materials were scarce, knitting wool proved invaluable and women knitting 'comforts' for the troops also made items for their families, from any colour and quality of wool available. Spare wool was never discarded and old adult garments were often unravelled, being reworked into children's clothes. As a form of camaraderie, women knitted in groups, even in air-raid shelters, or spent evenings at home darning and knitting, while listening to the radio.

Sourcing Fabrics and Clothes

The experience of acquiring dress-related items changed beyond recognition throughout the 150-year period covered by this book, reflecting the shift from a traditional domestic to industrial urban economy.

Our late-Georgian forebears had the means of acquiring all, or most, of their wardrobe requisites, although methods changed over time. In 1800, nearly all clothes (except for ready-made 'slops', cheap pre-fabricated garments initially produced in ports for sailors and travellers) were individually made-to-measure by hand, using lengths of material and all the requisite 'notions' (haberdashery). Around two-thirds of the population were country dwellers and in some districts there still operated the traditional system of itinerant jobbing weavers, who set up their looms in a client's parlour or barn, to weave into usable fabric domestically sourced wool or linen (flax) already spun into yarn by the women of the house. Otherwise, materials could be bought from various tradesmen, including travelling salesmen, pedlars and hawkers carrying large backpacks containing fabric lengths, thread, ribbons, sewing aids, even small dress items. Visiting many rural areas, itinerant operators offered goods of varying qualities and prices to suit all pockets, also extending credit to customers.

Additionally, by 1800 most villages and hamlets had their own grocery shop or general store supplying local farmers, farm workers, servants and other tradespeople, albeit sometimes trading from a makeshift outlet such as the pub or corner of a barn. Shopkeepers understood the needs of the local population and besides food, household goods and work tools, invariably textiles and haberdashery featured prominently among their merchandise, a brass rule set into the wooden counter for measuring out cloth. Material for women's gowns, spencer jackets, pelisses and other items could also be bought at fairs, market stalls and in country towns, where provincial retailers typically included drapers, mercers, hatters, boot- and shoe-makers and milliners. The millinery trade was not initially limited to ladies' hat-making, but traditionally supplied many small ready-made ladies' items including cloaks, aprons, stockings, gloves, caps and bonnets, as well as dress ornaments and trimmings. Some professional dressmakers also kept fashionable fabrics and all the necessary threads, fastenings and trimmings, while male tailors – who tended to work with woollen cloths and heavier-weight fabrics – usually stocked materials for men's coats and breeches, women's tailored riding and walking habits.

Cities, busy port towns and stylish spa and seaside resorts were well served with fashionable outlets, from large warehouses selling affordable merchandise to the general public, to prestigious specialist retailers. London – the acknowledged world centre of gentlemen's tailoring by the Regency era – and other locations frequented by high society such as Bath, Tunbridge Wells and Brighton gained new, elegant shopping areas that attracted seasonal visitors and catered for local residents. In the provincial towns that made up much of Britain's urban landscape in the early to mid-1800s, drapers, tailors and other fashion outlets boasted a surprisingly mixed clientele, according to Alison Topliss in *The Clothing Trade in Provincial England, 1800–1850*. Where retail establishments operated in stiff competition with one another, as they did in Worcester for example, respected tailors and drapers relied on patrons from various social backgrounds and actively welcomed working-class custom, advertising 'cheap wearing apparel'.

By the mid-1800s, reflecting the growing tide of industrialisation, improved communications and advancing mass-production of many textiles and garments, shopping practices were undergoing a marked change. Travelling salesmen still operated in some areas, but old-style pedlars and hawkers were giving way to tallymen; these traders also supplied goods on credit but were employed by shops, carrying samples and taking orders, returning at intervals for payment instalments. As woollen and cotton products from the new factories and mills of northern England and the Midlands multiplied and diversified, and as railway networks expanded across the country, manufacturers also sent out their own representatives, bringing an ever widening range of goods to provincial markets.

Some ready-made male clothes had been available since the 1700s, mainly in port towns, from 'show shops' or 'slop shops'

'The Linen Draper' from *The Book of English Trades*, 1824.

catering for sailors and voyagers needing basic outfits at short notice. These kinds of outlets, and the garment-making enterprises that supplied them, went on to form the backbone of the growing nineteenth-century ready-made clothing industry. Men's garments, becoming increasingly uniform during the 1800s and considerably more standardised in cut and style than women's complex outfits, were well-suited to early mass-production. Tailors and men's outfitters multiplied and by the turn of the twentieth century most tailoring companies, such as Austin Reed, founded in 1900, and Montague Burton's (1903), offered both made-to-measure and ready-to-wear services.

Another key fashion development of the period was the departmental, or department, store (also mentioned in Chapter 4). In addition to the large early-nineteenth-century warehouses and bazaars, by the mid-1800s onwards many local drapery businesses were expanding their premises and stocking more diverse fabrics, clothes, accessories and household goods; these would gradually develop into the vast department stores that dominated every mid- to late-Victorian high street. Women in particular frequented the dazzling emporia, many of which also featured tearooms, hairdressers, photography studios and other amenities, offering middle-class females a respectable shopping and social venue. Besides providing dedicated sales areas for every fashionable requirement over the generations, from mourning apparel to cosmetics, stores also offered bespoke garment making-up and alterations departments so that items purchased in-store, or elsewhere, could be fashioned to suit customers' individual requirements.

Many women's quality machine-made clothes were still hand-finished until after the First World War, and bespoke tailoring and dressmaking thrived until the mid-twentieth century. My maternal grandmother, a professional court dressmaker before marriage, always used a traditional mother-and-daughter dressmaking business for her own impeccable bespoke clothes, while bringing up five children in the 1920s and 1930s. However, female ready-to-wear fashion was also advancing significantly at this time, when growing simplicity of garment style, cheaper fabrics and improved sizing all aided mass-production of women's clothes. At the same time, popular retail outlets in the form of American-style multiple or chain stores were multiplying, beginning in the 1920s with Woolworths 'Threepenny and Sixpenny Stores' – shops for the masses, where even cheap diamond engagement rings could be purchased. Mail order, pioneered in the late 1800s, also came into its own during the first half of the twentieth century, bringing affordable fashion to all but the poorest in society.

Chapter 9

Caring for Clothes

Historically, dress items – whether professionally tailor-/dressmaker-made, shop-bought as new, acquired second-hand, or home-made – were considered valuable property; they had an intrinsic worth and, indeed, comprised most of the personal possessions owned by poorer ancestors. Clothes and accessories had to be kept dirt-free and in good repair if they were to last and if the wearer was to look neat and respectable. In prosperous households, ladies' maids and men's valets oversaw the maintenance of their employer's wardrobes and in middle-class homes there were servants to assist, while ordinary people largely cared for their own apparel. Whatever the arrangement, earlier generations knew exactly what garments were made of and how to look after them properly, for optimum wear.

Preserving Fine Apparel

The women, servants or others who took responsibility for clothing the household understood the qualities of different fabrics, selecting their cleaning methods accordingly. Until the 1920s, when artificial silk ('art silk' or rayon) became widely available, heralding a new era of synthetic drip-dry, non-iron fabrics, all textiles for clothing were woven from natural fibres: linen, cotton, silk and wool, or mixed fabrics containing different combinations of the above. Traditionally many women wore formal silk and velvet garments for dressy occasions; linen and cotton for relaxed summer wear, or coarser versions for workaday clothes; woollen-based fabrics for tailored winter clothes, outdoor sports and sometimes as underwear. Some clothing items were extremely difficult to clean, from diaphanous white muslins, through robust corsets to formal gowns with complex draperies. Frocks with fragile trimmings sometimes had to be unpicked before washing, then carefully sewn up again. Fine silk or velvet dresses could not be washed at all using water, so layers of underwear, including a shift/chemise, petticoats, separate washable white collars and detachable under-sleeves protected costly outer garment fabrics from direct bodily contact.

Walking outdoors in city streets or country lanes in floor-length Victorian and Edwardian garments inevitably attracted mud and debris, so immediately after wear clothes were shaken and dirt, dust and soot smuts thoroughly brushed from them, using clothes brushes. Some floor-length or trained gowns incorporated a fabric frill or ruffle sewn close to the lower edge of the skirt on the inside; called a *balayeuse*, this served to sweep up much of the dirt as the wearer walked, and was easily removed for cleaning, leaving the skirt hemline relatively unspoiled. A coat or jacket, waistcoat and trousers comprised the regular Victorian male suit, but apart from certain cotton and linen workwear, suits could not usually be washed in water and, like ladies' formal gowns, men's garments were brushed regularly at home. Beaver and felt hats were brushed too, as were leather shoes and boots. The hallstand once used in the downstairs hallway of many homes incorporated mirrors, shelves and hooks for different brushes for dusting off and smartening up clothes.

In the 1800s, there were no commercial dry-cleaners, only specialists who refurbished luxury items used for accessories and trimmings, such as lace, furs and feathered headdresses or boas. Some also offered professional dyeing services; early vegetable-based fabric dyes were often fugitive, prone to fading in bright light over time, so garments sometimes needed rejuvenating. Also, as we saw in Chapter 7, clothes were often professionally dyed black to serve as mourning attire.

If a lady's silk bodice or a gentleman's velvet smoking jacket became spotted or stained, for example with oil or grease, candle-wax, food, wine, tea or coffee, then women often followed traditional home recipes handed down through the family. Alternatively, popular periodicals and domestic handbooks published helpful household hints, for instance use of chemical solvents or natural products from larder or garden to remove diverse stains from various fabrics.

The Household Laundry

Although certain fragile fabrics and garments required dedicated cleaning methods, cotton towels, bed-linen and basic cotton and linen clothes were all washed in the normal manner, using soap and hot water. Typically these included all underclothes and nightwear, baby frocks, children's dresses and pinafores, men's shirts, women's cotton gowns, aprons, caps, collars and cuffs – literally hundreds of items in medium to large families. The frequency of washdays depended on the composition and financial status of the household, for the better off a family, the more changes of clean linen its members were likely to possess. Given the effort involved in hand-washing clothes, it was far easier to carry out occasional 'great washes' than frequent small washes. Hence, in affluent households whose residents owned dozens of shirts, shifts, drawers, stockings, handkerchiefs and so on, wash day occurred monthly, even quarterly, whereas in poorer homes, where nobody owned more than 'three of everything', laundry day was necessarily a weekly event.

"EMPIRE" WASHER AND WRINGER
SIMPLE,
ECONOMICAL,
EFFICIENT.

Prices of Washers :

30s.,   42s.,   50s.,

Wringers :

35s., and 45s.

ILLUSTRATED PROSPECTUS, with numerous Testimonials, and PHOTOGRAPH of MACHINE, free on application.

From T. H. BOXER, Commander, R.N., and Captain of "Chichester" Training Ship, Greenhithe.
8th September, 1876.

SIRS,—I have had one of your Washing Machines and Wringing Machines in use for six months, during which time it has had a severe test, not only in my own house, but I have washed over 200 boys' blankets, bed covers, &c., at a saving of 75 per cent., using our own water and not paying for labour ; calculating these two items in, I should think, on the whole, there would be a saving of 50 per cent. With this experience I can gladly recommend them.
Messrs. Wolstencroft & Co.   (Signed)   T. H. BOXER.

THOMAS WOLSTENCROFT & COMPANY
46, LUDGATE HILL, LONDON, E.C.

Advertisement from *Whitakers Almanack*, 1878.

Wash day usually began on a Monday, food for the day either prepared in advance over the weekend or assembled from left-over cold meat, pickles and pudding from Sunday dinner, negating the need to cook while contending with the laundry. Generally all capable females were involved in fetching and boiling water, rubbing, scrubbing, rinsing and wringing clothes. It was inevitably a wet, steamy and messy business and sometimes large aprons with separate sleeves, capacious overalls and protective overshoes or pattens were worn. Frequently the washing, drying and ironing stretched over several days, larger families often employing a general servant to assist, and/or hiring a local washerwoman. Men were rarely directly involved, yet husbands and sons knew when it was wash day. One Lancashire farmer, Farmer Valentine, even recorded each wash day in his (unpublished) diary covering the late 1870s, noting the weather conditions when clothes were hung out to dry.

The extent of domestic disruption depended on where clothes-washing operations took place. Large country houses usually had a dedicated wash house with sloping brick floors for water drainage, sometimes plumbed to supply hot and cold water directly to the washing tubs; some even had separate ironing and drying rooms or a special furnace-heated drying closet, teams of laundry maids undertaking the whole process. In town houses, washing might be carried out in the basement, where there was often a direct water supply. Some country cottages had a small lean-to wash house, the water heated by a copper, but in small two-up, two-down homes the laundry had to be done in the kitchen/parlour/general family room, among children, pets and all the paraphernalia of everyday life. Not surprisingly, those who could afford the modest expense sent their household washing out to a local laundry or professional laundress or washerwoman; for more about ancestors employed in this occupation, see Chapter 10.

A weekly or fortnightly hand-wash of numerous cotton and linen garments – 'the whites' – using soap and hot water was a laborious process. According to *The Workwoman's Guide* by A Lady (1838), a good washerwoman first examined each item, soaping soiled areas like collars and cuffs. She then hand-washed everything in warm soapy water, twice, items next being passed through the wringer or mangle, afterwards checked again for stubborn stains. For much of the 1800s, washing was carried out in a large oak or earthenware tub, with the aid of a washing 'dolly' – a three- or four-legged pole for 'possing' or pounding clothes – or the 'peggy tub', with a corrugated interior. So-called washing 'machines' comprising wooden boxes on legs that circulated clothes using a rocking or rotating movement were developed in the early 1800s, but they had to be hand-operated and were so heavy and cumbersome that servants refused to use them. Later, steam-driven versions appeared, but users disliked the 'new-fangled' apparatus. Early electric household washing machines developed in the 1920s, automatic versions in the 1930s, but only from mid-century did many homes acquire the new labour-saving appliances.

After initial hand-washing of linens, and further wringing or mangling, the washing was then boiled in a copper pot containing hot soapy water and simmered for an hour or more. Victorian soap was usually the basic yellow household variety, although white curd soap was sometimes employed on more delicate items. Traditionally soap was bought in large lumps, then divided into smaller bars and dissolved in boiling water to form a semi-liquid jelly that, when combined with hot water, produced a strong, soapy solution for immersing clothes. In 1884, Lever Brothers launched the first packaged and branded laundry soap, Sunlight Soap, which had a clear appearance. Some women used alternative detergents, such as paraffin, an excellent solvent for grease, and the soapwort plant, whose boiled leaves and flowers produce alkali.

Once linens were completely washed and boiled, they were generally rinsed in fresh hot water, then cold water, to remove any residual soap, soda or other cleaning agents. It was usual to add blue to the final rinse, which effectively turned yellowing fabrics into a more acceptable grey-white. Traditionally the blue was often smalt (ground cobalt glass) or small lumps of indigo and starch called 'stone blue', wrapped in a cloth bag and squeezed into, or drawn through the water, mixing it well, to avoid blue streaks in the linen (see coloured image No.14). To make linens even whiter, sometimes bleaches and softeners such as saltpetre and borax were added to the washing water. Eventually the washed linen would be of good colour and fresh-smelling. It would have taken many hours of hard labour, including constant lifting of wet, heavy clothes and filling, emptying and refilling of water tubs.

Woollen clothes, including warm flannel underwear and hand-knitted items, featured more prominently in fashionable dress from the late 1800s onwards and these were easily ruined in the wash. Hot water and soap alkalis caused shrinkage and yellowing, while over-wringing turned the soft, pliable woollen fibres into a stiff felt mass. Ideally woollens were plunged straight into a mixture of warm – never hot – soapy water and ammonia (a gentle bleach), then were drawn up and down and swirled about gently, before rinsing. Bright red flannel petticoats and other coloured garments were also washed separately, to avoid the transfer of dye and also to prevent fading or streaking the colours with harsh cleaning agents. In 1894, *Home Notes* recommended carefully hand-washing coloured flannels in a boiled solution of flour and water, with added suds, then rinsing three times in fresh water; other sources suggested soft rain water with a little ammonia, then rapid drying outdoors in the wind.

Starching, Drying and Ironing

Men's shirts were laundered with the family linen, but then required extra care and attention. Until the twentieth century, gentlemen's shirts were always white and needed effective starching. Various proprietary starches were manufactured by the 1800s, rice starch producing a good glazed finish, while corn starch could be made at home. Starch was always mixed with substances like paraffin, borax with milk, or white wax, to obtain the requisite shine that helped to prevent dirt attaching to the shirt fabric. Once diluted with boiling water, the front, neckband, collar and cuffs of the shirt were submerged, rubbed, left to dry, then dipped again into cold starch and rolled in a thick towel, to retain the damp until ironing. Women's white caps, aprons and frilled items were also stiffened, for example by combining white starch, borax and candle wax, the mixture then heated until it became a transparent jelly. Items were then dipped in, but had to be dried before ironing, whereas cold-starched articles could be ironed while still damp. It was also common to use a very thin, diluted water starch on all white cotton and linen underwear; this was thought to make washing easier and improve colour and overall appearance.

Wringers or mangles with large hand-powered rollers were used to squeeze water out of wet washing and to flatten and press large sheets and towels. Traditionally tall, heavy contraptions, these were a major domestic investment, often being shared by several households in a terrace or hamlet. Later Victorian models were smaller, cheaper and more adaptable, often attaching to the sides of wash tubs. After wringing, clothes were hung up to dry, either outside or indoors, draped on a clothes horse, airer or 'maiden' suspended from the ceiling. Ideally, washing was dried outdoors, for natural bleaching of whites in the sunshine, and to avoid an

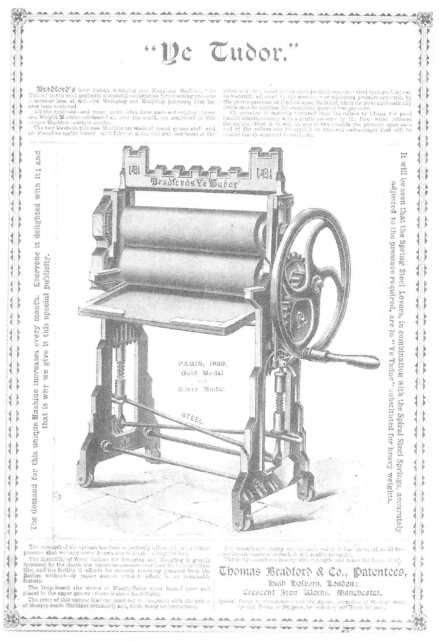

Mangle advertisement, 1889.

unhealthy damp atmosphere inside the house. Country women sometimes followed the time-honoured practice of laying washing out on the grass or on hedges, but usually it was pegged on lines. Drying clothes in built-up city neighbourhoods was more difficult; sometimes it was suspended from lines stretched across narrow alleyways, the rags of poorer families tied to sticks hung from tenement windows, storey above storey.

Ironing clothes was another time-consuming operation. Assorted articles needed different irons, the basic form a triangular flat-iron, heated on the stove or before the fire. Fashioned entirely from metal, it became extremely hot and had to be held using a padded holder. It was easy to scorch clothes, although experienced laundresses learned to gauge the temperature by holding the iron close to their cheek or spitting on it. Flat-irons also became sooty from the fire and attracted residual starch from clothes, so had to be cleaned constantly; however, when used correctly on a board or a clean table, they were effective for large expanses like the bodies of shirts and petticoats.

The other traditional iron was the box-iron, hollow and filled with hot coals or metal bricks. Less liable to mark or scorch, these were preferable for fragile garments and decorative details like dainty collars. Many female items, from caps to petticoats, were ornamented with rows of frills and keeping these in shape required special goffering or 'gauffering' irons. Men's shirts were quite specialised too and a purpose-designed board called a 'bosom-board' was sometimes used – a wooden board 1ft wide and 1½ft long, covered in thick flannel and a clean cotton fitted slip.

In 1882, an 'electric flatiron' was patented in the United States, but few British homes had reliable mains electricity before the 1920s, many considerably later. In 1938, Morphy Richards began to manufacture modern electric irons with electrical cord and temperature control. As sales surged after the Second World War, this represented a new age of labour-saving electrical equipment that would help our mothers and grandmothers with wash day.

Storing Clothes

When clothes were not being worn they were stored in various ways, depending on an individual's or family's circumstances and the nature of their home. Following tradition, in the Georgian era clothes were generally stored in personal baskets, chests and trunks. Ideally these portable receptacles were lockable and during the 1800s they were typically used by domestic servants and other working people, at home or when working away. However, many poorer people did not even possess these basic storage boxes – or the clothes to put in them, even if they had the space

February, 1927   *The Ladies'* HOME JOURNAL

The New *U*nderthings~~~

Not extravagant if you protect them from Two Enemies

IN cut and in color, underthings are as important from a style point of view as outerthings. The new slips and step-ins of crepe de chine, myriad-tinted—the ravishing negligees of soft silks and laces demand as much care as that you give your prettiest chiffons, your printed silks.

When you wash these filmy, delicate underthings that you adore, *two unseen enemies* threaten to rob them of their daintiness. That's why most women never risk their lovely silks—they use Lux instead!

The first enemy is rubbing with cake soap. The soft bloom of chiffon and crepe de chine is destroyed by rubbing. *The second enemy* you must avoid is the free alkali in most soaps—regardless of whether they are flakes, chips or cakes. Alkali fades delicate colors, cuts the life of dainty fabrics in half.

With Lux you defeat these two deadly enemies! Lux contains no alkali—*nothing that can injure.* With it there is no destructive rubbing. Just sparkling, cleansing suds, safe for anything that is safe in water alone.

Department stores estimate that in the last ten years Lux has saved American women a billion dollars in the protection of delicate fabrics! Lever Bros. Co., Cambridge, Mass.

LUX

Lux advertisement from *The Ladies' Home Journal*, 1927.

indoors. In labouring households, breeches, trousers, stockings and the like might be hung on a line indoors or suspended from a nail on the wall. Other clothing was wrapped in cloth, or folded and laid down on a table overnight, the same items usually put straight back on again the next day. Drying garments that had become soaked in the rain or moist with perspiration was near-impossible in damp, poorly ventilated homes, but still they were worn day in, day out by labouring families; unless used directly after washing and ironing, everyday workwear, especially linen and cotton items, must generally have had a grubby, creased appearance. 'Sunday best' clothes were, of course, usually safely stored in the pawnshop.

Otherwise, during the nineteenth century both wardrobes and chests of drawers started appearing in middle-class homes. Underwear and nightwear often amounted to many articles and these could be kept on shelves in linen closets or drawers, in individual bedrooms in larger houses, along with towels and bed-linen. Sometimes items stored together were carefully marked, making them easily identifiable among piles of similar-looking folded cotton, linen or flannel. The woman of the house, or her servants, had to make sure that cupboards were not damp, or clothes quickly became mildewed; unlike in labouring homes, garments were also only put away when clean and the starch washed out, so as not to attract insect pests – moth grubs were especially partial to articles treated with food starch.

When clothes were being put away for a length of time (for example at the end of each season), they had to be protected from both the light and dust, garments of different colours being kept separate too. For this reason, many articles like ladies' dresses and men's suits were individually wrapped in cloth or paper, small items like children's gloves and woollen stockings perhaps stored in well-labelled calico bags. The most elaborate Victorian and Edwardian gowns were sometimes unpicked and laid flat, while velvet and silk items had to be very carefully preserved without any creasing occurring: tissue paper was even inserted under buttons on some articles to prevent pressure on delicate materials.

Victorian cupboard-like wardrobes with shelves and dedicated hanging space encouraged the hanging up of good clothes, thereby reducing the need for some of the above rituals, although the modern coat-hanger was not known before the 1890s, and, according to some historians, not widely used until the early 1900s. Some wardrobe hanging compartments were fitted with brass rails, but users found that integral hangers could not be removed from the rail. Instead, nails and rows of pegs – or drawers and shelves – were all familiar methods of storing clothes in many of our predecessors' homes until the twentieth century. When suburban property ownership grew common between the wars, one of the first sets of furniture that a couple might save up to purchase was the modern 'bedroom suite' comprising sideboard, wardrobe and dressing-table.

Chapter 10

Clothing Industry Work

Throughout the nineteenth and early-twentieth centuries, many of our forebears earned their living in the fashion and clothing arena, carrying out highly skilled, or simpler but important tasks involved in the production or preservation of textiles, garments and dress-related items. This chapter is not an exhaustive survey of all relevant industries between 1800 and 1950; that would require many books and indeed some aspects have already been explored in other Pen & Sword titles: see, for example, *Tracing Your Textile Ancestor*s by Vivien Teasdale (2009) and *Tracing Your Trade & Craftsman Ancestors* by Adele Emm (2015). Rather, this is a brief introduction to some of the main regional trades, followed by consideration of under-researched, chiefly female working-class occupations.

Regional Manufactures

The manufacture of cloth for use in clothing, bedding, and other purposes was a long-established British industry, the climate ideal for producing woollen, linen and, later, cotton goods. Before the Industrial Revolution, the textile business was a cottage industry, carried out in many communities, in small workshops or at home, by artisans skilled in spinning, weaving and dyeing. When new technological inventions from the mid- to late 1700s onwards facilitated the mechanisation of textile production, items that had traditionally been individually hand-crafted now began to be produced in multiples, by machinery installed in large mills and factories. Advances in manufacturing did not occur everywhere, nor simultaneously, there remained significant regional differences; however, by 1800 the process of industrialisation was well underway, with textiles, especially cotton goods, at the heart of the expanding economy.

The surge in British textile production during the early to mid-1800s, especially in parts of northern England and the Midlands, was so

Cotton weaving shed from *Lancashire's Great Industry* postcard series, c.1909.

significant that in the 1851 census, after agricultural work and domestic service, cotton manufacturing came third as an occupation, employing over half-a-million workers. Cotton mill and factory workers were based mainly in Manchester (dubbed 'Cottonopolis'), Oldham and Bolton in Lancashire and in the Nottingham area. The rise of the English cotton industry is a much-covered subject and family historians with cotton-worker ancestors should refer to dedicated sources and consult local records for more information.

Woollen textiles, created from the natural fleeces of sheep, had been important manufactures since the Middle Ages, and during the Industrial Revolution, Yorkshire became chiefly associated with the production of woollen cloth. Much woollen manufacturing was centred on Bradford, West Yorkshire – a market town with a modest population of 6,000 in 1801; this had escalated to 400,000 inhabitants by 1901, the city being dubbed 'Worstedopolis' – the 'worsted' or 'wool capital of the world'. These figures reflect both the nation's rising population, and continuing migration into manufacturing centres as earlier generations of our families moved away from depressed rural areas, seeking regular work.

Another key fashion-related industry was knitting, early knitted items mainly being caps and hose (see also Chapter 8). Commercial hand-knitting was established in Nottinghamshire and Leicestershire by the sixteenth century, with stocking-frame knitting advancing during the 1600s. By the nineteenth century, following refinement of production processes and reflecting changing fashion, close-fitting knitted cloth items included stockings, pantaloons, vests, shirts and mittens. Throughout the 1800s around 90 per cent of Britain's 20,000 or more stocking frames were located in the East Midlands, with Nottinghamshire generally specialising in cotton goods, Derbyshire in silk and Leicestershire in worsted. Other important centres of framework knitting included the Scottish borders, Tewkesbury in Gloucestershire and Godalming in Surrey.

Hand-frame knitting was carried out at home, providing low-paid piecework for numerous families living in local villages, until large-scale factory production using power-driven machines transformed the industry in the late 1800s. Advancing mechanisation meant loss of work; the number of men employed in hosiery-producing areas was halved by the end of the century, but some found alternative employment in the Midlands-based boot and shoe industry. Footwear was traditionally hand-sewn by outworkers but manufacture changed when large-scale factories entered the scene in around the mid-1800s. Large boot- and shoe-factories and smaller workshops remained a major employer of local people until British factories relocated overseas in the twentieth century. Many of our ancestors worked in this industry, which was largely based in Leicester, Northampton and Stafford; additionally, small businesses where boots and shoes could be bought and repaired continued everywhere, well into the 1900s.

Throughout the nineteenth and first-half of the twentieth centuries, hats were important dress accessories – considered essential for a respectable appearance, as well as fashion items – and the manufacture of headwear was carried out in different geographical areas. Traditionally the process of making expensive, formal men's hats such as the Regency round hat, early prototypes of the 'top hat' and the tall mid-nineteenth-century stove-pipe hat required imported beaver fur, and water, so centres of hat-making included London and ports such as Liverpool, Bristol and Exeter. Later, as beaver became scarce, coney (rabbit) and wool were more usually used in felt hat-making; Warwickshire arose as a centre, but most important in the Victorian and Edwardian periods were Stockport and Denton, close to Manchester.

Straw hat-making was a separate industry to felt hat manufacturing, the making of straw bonnets and hats being a recognised trade in

Bedfordshire, Buckinghamshire and Hertfordshire by the late-seventeenth century. In many local villages, children learned to plait straw from a young age, contributing to the making of hats and other goods including boxes, baskets and toys. Dunstable Bonnets were already famous by 1800, the industry expanding rapidly during the Napoleonic Wars due to shortage of supplies, traditionally imported from Italy. Trades associated with straw plaiting and straw hat-making spread throughout the south-east Midlands and beyond, to parts of East Anglia, Middlesex, the West Country, even Orkney. In some areas, straw work continued at the small-scale cottage-industry level, employing many home-workers, while from the mid-1800s until the early 1900s, London, Luton, St Albans and Dunstable thrived as large mechanised straw hat manufacturing centres.

Other fashion industries that provided work for our forebears in different parts of the country include glove-making, gloving centres being established, for example in Somerset and Dorset, by the 1300s/1400s. Over the centuries, various materials were used for making gloves and different production centres emerged; for instance, framework knitted gloves and mittens using cotton or silk yarns were manufactured in the Midlands, chiefly around Nottingham and Leicester. In the 1770s, the famous glove-making company, Dents of Worcester was founded, employing over half of Britain's glovers by 1800 – in excess of 30,000

'A Plaiting School' – engraving from *The Queen*, 9 November 1861.

workers at its peak. Glove-making also surged elsewhere, for instance in Yeovil, where the industry employed over 10,000 workers from Somerset and nearby Dorset villages by the mid-1800s. During the nineteenth century, women's and men's glove-making work also became increasingly demarcated; men and older boys monopolised the skilled dressing and cutting of leather, while females did much of the sewing. Thousands of women and children undertook piecework at home, stitching and finishing gloves to order, for local manufacturers.

In many parts of Britain, home-working on small dress-related items continued well into the machine age, while in other districts mechanisation occurred early, drawing our ancestors into the business of mass-production in larger workshops and factories. Occupational circumstances depended on the nature of the industry and the geographical area. For example, making delicate artificial flower ornaments for fashionable ladies' hats was often a low-paid job carried out on a piecework basis by women and children, including London's poorest East End slum-dwellers.

Some regions, chiefly in southern England, remained predominantly agricultural, with few large-scale mills or factories churning out mass-produced consumer goods, yet fashion-related manufactures were often important local trades. For example, as Rachel Worth explains in *Discover Dorset: Dress & Textiles*, Dorset, still a rural county today, produced many local manufactures, from cloth, to buttons and lace. There the long-established local woollen cloth industry still thrived during the 1800s, centred mainly on Sturminster Newton and Lyme Regis, while flax was grown for making into linen cloth well into the nineteenth century. Local silk production struggled due to French competition from the 1820s, but silk throwing, and silk weaving at Sherborne survived into the twentieth century. Particularly important in Dorset were haberdashery and dressmaking aids – items essential for the making and trimming of garments and accessories. The local glove-making and 'buttony' (button-making) industries relied on the handicraft skills of generations of women and children working at home.

Hand-made bobbin-lace (or 'pillow lace') was a specialist local craft practised in many Dorset and Devon villages and elsewhere in the West Country, as well as in Bedfordshire, Buckinghamshire and Northamptonshire. A cottage industry dating back to the late 1500s, in the nineteenth century it was still common to see women sitting outside their doorways in summer, working at their lace. Fine hand-made lace, highly skilled, labour-intensive work, was made into exquisite collars, cuffs, bodice panels and other fashionable trimmings for luxury dress; however, like other old craft-based trades, the introduction of cheaper machine-made lace during the 1800s contributed to the decline of this traditional handiwork.

To sum up this brief survey, large numbers of our ancestors and more recent relatives, whether out-workers or employees who travelled daily to work at a nearby workshop or mill, were engaged in various occupations relating to dress. Their position would almost entirely have depended on where they lived, for in certain districts small-scale trades flourished, or people worked at home for large local employers, while elsewhere

Postcard photograph of elderly pillow-lace maker, early 1900s.

the workplace was an urban factory. Some trades were highly localised and unique, such as the production of Manx cloth on the Isle of Man, or Fair Isle knitwear. The scale of clothing and textile-related work still at the turn of the twentieth century (by when some traditional industries were declining) was highlighted in Bartholomew's *Survey Gazetteer of the British Isles* (Newnes, 1904), which drew on the 1901 census. In that year, the occupational category 'Textiles, Clothing & Food' accounted for at least 20 per cent of the working population in many counties, including Berkshire, Essex and Somerset. Elsewhere, the proportion of textiles, clothing and food workers was significantly higher; for instance, in Lancashire, London and Norfolk about one-quarter of the local population; in Cheshire, Nottinghamshire and Yorkshire around one-third; in Northamptonshire 42 per cent; and in Leicestershire and Rutland combined, almost half of local people worked in textiles, clothing and food.

Some regional industries focusing on certain products or brands of apparel were – and are – renowned. Local manufacturing may well have helped to shape and raise the status of a town, even inspiring the name of its football team (for instance Luton Town Football Club – 'The Hatters').

Some provided employment for generations of the same families, who frequently married work colleagues, their children later entering the same occupation. Readers are likely to be aware of ancestors engaged in, say, the Lancashire cotton industry, Northampton boot-making or the Dorset/Somerset/Worcester gloving trade. Further research into their work and lives can be conducted using specialist published sources – of which there are many – or by consulting dedicated record collections in archives and museums local to relevant areas. Some museums are dedicated largely or solely to a trade, such as Hat Works in Stockport or Allhallows Museum of Lace and Antiquities in Honiton. Using their resources and paying a visit is a perfect way to investigate past family members' skills and learn more about their working lives.

Dressmakers and Seamstresses

As outlined in Chapter 8, generations of women in our families learned to sew as soon as they could handle needle and thread. Home sewing was a traditional domestic skill and until at least the mid-twentieth century typically the females of a house made and repaired some of the family's clothes. For many, simple sewing or more advanced dressmaking was also a crucial means of earning an income, especially in the nineteenth century when women enjoyed few work opportunities outside the home. Following tradition, or through sheer necessity, many of our mothers, grandmothers, great-grandmothers and their predecessors turned their talents into an occupation, as professional dressmakers and seamstresses.

Women first entered the needlework trade in large numbers during the Napoleonic Wars (1803–15), when they were employed to sew ships' sails and military uniforms. Females were cheaper for the authorities to engage and considered more dextrous and less liable than men to 'combination' (early moves towards unionisation). As the nineteenth century advanced, demand grew in other areas, especially the expanding market for economical ready-made clothes. Broadly, nineteenth- and early-twentieth-century needlewomen fell into two main categories: those who underwent apprenticeships or training and entered 'respectable' private dressmaking concerns (which varied widely from refined, upmarket establishments to unexceptional local businesses), and those who did low-paid piecework for large employers, often as home outworkers – essentially sweated labour.

The more fortunate girls who received formal dressmaking instruction were typically daughters from professional, clerical, trade, artisan or farming families. Being apprenticed sometimes as young as 12, more usually from around 14 years old and upwards, they trained for a minimum of two or three, sometimes several years, although apprenticeship terms varied; arrangements might be informal if the training was with a relative or family friend. Otherwise, instruction with a professional garment-maker could be an expensive option, not open to all; an annual premium of £10 – £15 per annum to cover living costs was not unusual by the late 1800s, while the young apprentices themselves often worked long hours for low or no pay.

An occupation in dressmaking was hard and could be unpredictable, often seasonal, but attainment of high standards could secure a desirable position, for example with a prestigious court dressmaker or 'costumier' catering for a wealthy clientèle. As city department stores developed in the mid- to late 1800s and early 1900s, many young women were also employed as dressmakers in their making-up and alterations departments – respectable jobs, yet still involving long hours. Sometimes personal

A Dressmaker's Workroom in the West End of London: anonymous print dated 1858.

business opportunities arose; with some capital and useful connections, a skilled professional might hope to launch her own venture. Many local dressmaking establishments or 'madame shops', run independently, or jointly by sisters or mother-and-daughter partnerships, earned a trusted reputation in their neighbourhood, providing a decent career and reasonable livelihood.

At the other end of the scale were needlewomen from a lower social class – those from less fortunate backgrounds, or who had fallen on hard times. Large numbers went out to work as seamstresses, sewing for unscrupulous employers in crowded, ill-lit and poorly ventilated workrooms, sometimes even living on the premises, in the same conditions. At this level, many women experienced digestive, respiratory and rheumatic complaints and eye problems, with much of their work being carried out in the gloom, failing sight exacerbated when handling black mourning fabric. Women also earned considerably less than male tailors doing comparable work; residential needlewomen might be paid between £12 and £30 per annum, depending on skill (roughly on a par with domestic servants); yet they needed to look presentable when dealing with customers, so employers might retain part of their wages to cover clothing.

The gruelling hours (up to eighteen hours a day at busy times of the year), low pay and unsatisfactory working environment in wretched Victorian sweatshops did not go unnoticed. *The Song of the Shirt*, a famous poem by Thomas Hood (1843), began:

> With fingers weary and worn,
> With eyelids heavy and red,
> A woman sat in unwomanly rags,
> Plying her needle and thread –
> Stitch! Stitch! Stitch!
> In poverty, hunger, and dirt,
> And still with a voice of dolorous pitch
> She sang 'The Song of the Shirt!'

In 1851, social investigator Henry Mayhew observed in *London Labour and the London Poor* that some needlewomen were so desperately poor that they sometimes turned to prostitution. Since few females are actually recorded as such in official documents, such comments have led to the erroneous assumption that the term 'dressmaker' is literally a euphemism for 'prostitute'. More accurately, in an age when female employment opportunities outside the home were severely limited, before the welfare state any poor, vulnerable woman without sufficient income to meet basic living expenses may have turned to earning money however she could. This did not only apply to seamstresses or lower grades of dressmaker, but to any unsupported female without employment or working in a desperately low-paid job; presumably for most of those needlewomen who took that route it was a last resort – generally the exception, rather than the rule.

Some of our poor needleworking ancestors were widows, or married women whose husbands were unable or unwilling to work. Needing to juggle employment with childcare and other domestic responsibilities, many working-class housewives undertook sewing at home as seamstresses or pieceworkers for local clothing manufacturers or wholesalers, making or finishing garments, from suits, blouses, and dresses, to shirts and nightwear. This type of outwork, involving working for diverse employers, existed nationwide, although the highest concentration of female homeworkers occurred in geographical areas where male wages were notoriously low, or where men's jobs were mainly casual or seasonal; also in places where there was no other employment for women, creating a surplus of female labour.

In *A Hidden Workforce: Homeworkers in England, 1850–1985*, Shelley Pennington and Belinda Westover explain how, during the nineteenth century, London, Essex and Bristol all developed as major centres for homeworking in the light clothing industry. As consumer demand expanded and manufacturing increased and diversified, certain goods became associated with particular locations. For instance, Leeds was best-known for woollen outer clothing; raincoat manufacture was strongest in and around Manchester; miscellaneous dress trades operated in the West Midlands, South Wales, Bristol and Nottingham areas; while Norwich, Colchester and other eastern districts specialised in tropical wear. Wars also affected the kinds of sewing piecework available at different points in time; for example, thousands of female homeworkers served the Colchester tailoring factories commissioned to produce millions of military uniforms during the First World War.

Garment manufacturers, wholesalers and retailers relied enormously on the predominantly female home-based labour force. Material would be issued to middlemen – agents or 'mistresses' – who divided the cloth up into smaller quantities, distributing these to the home-workers, along with instructions as to what was required. The work could then be fitted in around family commitments and household tasks – no doubt a difficult undertaking in the average chaotic, overcrowded working-class home. Further, because of the history of sewing as a traditional female skill and the circumstances in which much of it was carried out, sewing was inextricably linked to unpaid domestic work and few employers paid a realistic wage; for instance, the Select Committee on Sweating, 1888 discovered that an outworker making an entire coat for a wholesale firm earned just 7*d* or 8*d*; later, during the First World War, a Colchester pieceworker received 2*s* 6*d* for making one dozen army shirts.

Homeworkers also had to provide their own needles and thread, pay for heating and lighting and arrange to return the finished articles at their own expense; if completed work was pronounced sub-standard or delivered late, they incurred a fine. The middlemen also took their own cut of every transaction. Many outworkers not only struggled financially, but often worked in unsanitary conditions, for domestic environments were not covered by the successive Factory Acts that eventually began to regulate official workplaces. Whether trying to support their family alone, or working to supplement a meagre household income, tragically many of the seamstresses and lowly dressmakers in our families a century or more ago were trapped by poverty and lack of opportunity within the system of sweated labour that supported the clothing industry.

Home piecework was eventually affected by changing technology, notably the advent of mechanised sewing from around the mid-1800s. In time, seamstresses working at home were expected to provide their own sewing machines, but these being initially expensive, often women pooled resources, sharing a hand-crank or treadle machine, until eventually the price of domestic machines reduced and rental or hire purchase arrangements came into place. Domestic sewing machines could speed up the rate of piecework, at least for certain tasks; so while some clothing factories and workshops used machinery operators to produce garments on an industrial scale, other employers continued to use outworkers, for as long as the supply of cheap labour continued. Mechanisation did not displace homeworkers, but effectively perpetuated the piecework system, which continued well into the twentieth century.

Humanitarian concern for exploited needlewomen had been growing since the mid-1800s, various philanthropic organisations being established that tried to encourage shorter working hours and reorganisation of the trade. There were also a number of regional associations, all of these initiatives being followed in the later nineteenth century by needleworking cooperatives, via which women began to campaign for their own rights. Feminists were active from the 1890s in exposing the appalling conditions in which many women worked and by the turn of the century sweating was of both public and trade union interest.

Eventually statutory protection was introduced for all workers labouring in the sweated trades – men and women. The Trade Boards Act of 1909 enabled the setting up of boards to regulate wages in any branch of a trade in which income was particularly low. By 1913, when minimum rates were eventually in place, some of the worst evils of sweated work were diminishing, but this came too late for generations of our ancestors. Clementina Black's survey of married women's work, published in 1915, revealed the perpetuation of vast differences in pay and conditions between the poorer workers, exploited by middlemen, and highly skilled dressmakers, who lived a comparatively comfortable life.

The decennial census returns reveal that large numbers of our ancestors were engaged in one or another aspect of the clothing manufacturing trades – a vast category of predominantly (but not exclusively) female industry. Needleworker, dressmaker and seamstress (or its alternative spelling, sempstress) are common occupational terms, others including sewers, tailors, milliners, clothiers, and garment makers. Some women were listed under more specialised titles denoting the particular items that they made, such as stay-makers, hosiery manufacturers, garter-makers, glovers, shirt-makers, straw bonnet-sewers, and boot- and shoe-stitchers. Various related needle trades also crop up, for example button and hook-and-eye carding, umbrella-covering, and embroideress. Entries reflect the particular garments and accessories that our ancestors were engaged in making at various points in time, as well as the march of industrialisation; those of the late 1800s and early 1900s demonstrate the accelerating role of the sewing machine, with nearly 5,000 women recorded as sewing machinist (or similar) in 1881, around 24,000 by 1911.

Washerwomen and Laundry Workers

In Chapter 9 we saw how earlier generations washed and cleaned various types of clothes; this was an arduous task, especially on 'wash day', and for centuries it was common for poorer people to earn money by helping others with their laundry. Hand-laundry work was chiefly a female occupation, industry workers usually referred to as washerwomen or laundresses. Many of our humble working-class female forebears will have laboured in such a role, if not regularly, then periodically, whenever the need arose. Traditional hand-laundry services lingered on in many areas, although more recent generations may have worked in modern, well-equipped mechanised laundries.

Historically the social elite always employed servants or professional washerwomen to undertake the household laundry, grand urban residences and country houses operating dedicated laundry rooms staffed by laundry maids. During the 1800s, as the population rose and many Britons grew wealthier, outsourcing the washing became common practice, both to relieve the domestic burden and to present an appearance of gentility; hence the middle classes and better-off working-class families also sent their laundry out, or engaged extra help at home. The frequency of the laundry directly reflected the quantity of clothes that a household possessed, thereby also indicating social and economic status; the most privileged families typically favoured large-scale quarterly laundry operations, while every four to six weeks was common in middle-class homes. Members of most ordinary families had only one, two or three sets of linen – usually only sufficient for a weekly wash.

As outlined in Chapter 9, before mechanised washing appliances, hand-washing was a massive undertaking, involving many laborious processes. A professional washerwoman or laundress might be required to handle all of a family's washing, including linen, cotton and some flannel items: men's shirts, baby clothes, nightwear, undergarments, aprons, caps, kerchiefs, work smocks and simple day frocks, household bedlinen, towels and washable furniture covers and curtains. Often physical space was limited when doing the washing; small-scale laundry operations often occurred in a basement, in the laundress's own home or in her customer's residence, causing considerable disruption to domestic life.

Typically a batch of hand laundry took about four to five days for a professional laundress to complete, the soiled items gathered from customers on Monday/Tuesday and returned, clean and ironed, on Friday/Saturday. The collected garments were first marked, sorted then washed in the manner usual for each item, according to fabric and colour. Hand-operated wringers squeezed water out of sodden washing and mangles with large rollers flattened larger items like sheets. Clothes were then dried outdoors, in bright light if possible, so that whites could be naturally bleached. Country washerwomen sometimes laid out washing on the grass or hedges; other laundresses used washing lines and some suburban laundries had special drying grounds.

Advertisement
for Sunlight Soap,
*Illustrated London
News*, 1902.

With washing and ironing being quite separate operations, independent washerwomen and the laundresses employed by small 'workshop' or 'hand' laundries needed competence in both processes. Washing was a basic working-class domestic chore, daughters learning from their mothers by helping out at home, while workhouse and orphanage girls were usually taught laundry techniques, to prepare them for future working life. Ironing was more skilled, yet in the 1800s there existed only limited training; occasionally ironers followed a three-month 'apprenticeship' and young girls were sometimes taken on as 'learners', but most adult women already had laundry experience, or learned on the job.

Traditional hand-laundry apparatus changed little during the nineteenth century, inventions like early manual washing 'machines' being cumbersome and widely unpopular. Wringers and mangles improved during the Victorian era, old versions being large, heavy contraptions often kept outdoors, while new, smaller models conveniently attached to wash tubs. A mangle was the most substantial item of requisite laundry equipment, before the industry became mechanised. Some professional laundresses purchased mangles to help with client work, also doing mangling for neighbours, charging one or two pence per load. Generally, older women often worked as 'manglers', especially widows; if a woman's husband died, it was common for neighbours and friends to club together and buy her a mangle, enabling her to earn a living.

Otherwise, with comparatively little expertise or equipment required, many of our poorer ancestors did laundry work as a regular job, or took in washing periodically in times of need. It was one of the few means by which uneducated women could earn an income; often they were the wives of men who were sick, indisposed, or who worked seasonally, their laundry-work wages supplementing or generating the family income; many others were impoverished widows. Victorian and Edwardian hand-washers typically earned 2s to 2s 6d per day, ironers (generally pieceworkers) 3s to 3s 6d, plus beer. Itinerant washerwomen visiting customers' homes generally received just 1s or 1s 6d per day, but were also given meals, perhaps food scraps to take home, even cast-off clothes for their children.

Hand-laundry work was an unpleasant, menial occupation – laborious and exhausting. Premises were often makeshift, cramped and poorly ventilated, the hot, steamy atmosphere frequently helping to spread consumption, bronchial complaints and rheumatism. The physical effort involved in shifting wet loads between tubs, hand-operating heavy equipment and kneading, squeezing and wringing water-laden washing was also intense. Although washerwomen could work part-time, shifts might be as long as eighteen hours, some women working an eighty-hour week. The most financially needy laboured the longest, until they could literally no longer stand, hence varicose veins and painful leg ulcers were also common ailments. Beer was often provided as part-payment, evidently keeping some women going well into old age, for census records name many octogenarian and older laundresses. Inevitably, the image of the archetypal washerwoman was that of an unkempt, uneducated, coarse-mannered woman; tough and hard-working, she was also capable, often the main family bread-winner.

Throughout the nineteenth and early-twentieth centuries, professional laundering was chiefly carried out by independent washerwomen, or by small workshop laundries employing local women. Traditional organisation and work methods persisted after mechanisation had transformed many other industries, although a few laundries began to use machinery in the late 1850s and 1860s, especially those specialising in large flat items for institutions and businesses. Gradually, more commercial laundries were established in key locations like London, university towns, popular spa and seaside resorts and major port cities – all places with large, shifting or seasonal populations requiring substantial laundry services. During the later 1800s, demand continued to grow well beyond domestic laundry, with department stores, hotels and restaurants, shipping lines, railways, government offices and large businesses placing lucrative contracts with new factory-sized laundries. Once municipal water supplies became reliable, the chief technological shift was towards vast steam-operated laundries, a trend that escalated between the 1890s and the First World War, even small workshops adopting more modern machinery.

Large factory laundries were often male-run, although from the early 1900s extensive training was also offered to middle-class ladies seeking managerial positions. There was increasing division of labour and a growing hierarchy of roles. Modern laundry work also attracted more young women than previously, although industrial accidents caused by dangerous unguarded machinery were now the main occupational hazards. Working conditions and wages slowly improved, with strengthening union presence and Trade Board minimum wage rates. But early incomes varied; only after 1919 did some wages improve, followed by a boom period and increased holiday entitlements during the Second World War, when the industry became crucial to the war effort. In 1945, an estimated 1,800 to 2,500 commercial laundries operated throughout Britain, employing some 127,500 to 190,000 staff. Yet this did not include the many independent laundresses who still took in washing or helped private households, their numbers unknown.

Even though some of our washerwomen or laundry-worker ancestors were never officially noted, some records do exist. The occupation is usually indicated in census returns as laundress, laundry worker or washerwoman, occasionally 'goes out washing', 'takes in washing at home', or 'washing and charring'. Reflecting changes in the industry, later censuses often add qualifying details like laundress servant, steam laundress, head laundress domestic. Evidently some of our ancestors recorded on censuses operated from home or at local premises, but others lived at institutional addresses including asylums, workhouses and orphanages, presumably as laundress inmates or residential staff.

Chapter 11

Fashion Heirlooms

Many of us are fortunate to possess tangible evidence of historical fashion in the form of inherited family heirlooms. Some are carefully preserved personal articles once treasured by ancestors and lovingly handed down the generations; others may be unexpected discoveries that speak in various ways of our predecessors' relationship with dress.

Costume Keepsakes

In the past it was common to keep and squirrel away important or unique items of clothing, perhaps because they had been painstakingly hand-made and/or were intrinsically valuable, held powerful, emotive memories of a particular event, or were intended to be passed on to others for future wear. Among the most popular clothing keepsakes to survive in today's family collections are babies' long white christening gowns. Obviously, these were initially intended for single-occasion use, but being special, decorative and often expensive items, generally they were put aside for wear by subsequent babies. Although available ready-made in shops and through mail order by the late 1800s, traditionally long christening or baptismal robes in muslin or other fine fabrics were painstakingly made at home, often by the baby's mother. Intricately hand-embroidered or otherwise embellished with thread, lace or delicate white-work, the hours of skilled workmanship represented devotion to the tiny being whose first public outing would be remembered in association with that very garment. Surviving christening gowns often display similar stylistic features and can be hard to date precisely; most will have originated in the Victorian or Edwardian period, and may have been worn by a number of infants over many years.

Also common among clothing heirlooms are bridal costumes; special white gowns with their accompanying headdresses and veils, Victorian bridegrooms' white wedding waistcoats, and stylish coloured silk or velvet costumes made for fashionable brides. Old wedding dresses in particular

have become part of a continuing
tradition in some families, the layers
of delicate material symbolising
timeless romance and seemingly
bestowing good luck on each new
bride. Sometimes part of an earlier
wedding costume is incorporated
into a more up-to-date ensemble, for
example an exquisite antique lace
veil, easily adapted and providing
the 'something old' element of the
proverbial marriage outfit. Wearing a
precious item that previously belonged
to a beloved mother, grandmother or
more distant predecessor also honours
their memory in a uniquely personal
way.

Mourning apparel is another
category of dress that sometimes
survives the passage of time. Macabre,
perhaps, to be reminded of death
and bereavement, but the Victorians

Blue crepe going-away outfit worn
by Dorothy Murton (née Wright) in
March 1952.

and Edwardians were nothing if not pragmatic; in their day such
garments were often intended to be reused. As we saw in Chapter 7,
mourning dress was a key element of high fashion; formal black fabrics
and trimmings could be handsome and costly – not to be readily cast
aside. It was also relatively straightforward to alter the style of existing
clothes when necessary, so mourning clothes may have been reused more
than once over the years. Muted half-mourning colours, soft greys and
mauves, were also fashionable at various points in time. Victorian brides
in mourning often wore such shades, these garments often appealing to
later generations.

Some clothing keepsakes do not fall within the common categories of
birth, marriage and death, but may be more random survivals – favourite
accessories, perhaps, or other dress items considered important in the
past. In my family, two moth-eaten old 1920s'-1940s' fox fur stoles
belonging to my grandmother and godmother were passed down through
my mother to me; impossible to wear now, presumably they were kept
as hard-earned, relatively costly fashion items, considered status symbols

in their day. Other survivals include faded evening gowns and other eccentric clothes kept for children's dressing-up activities, or heirlooms with special sentimental value, from wedding going-away outfits to a child's first pair of shoes.

Jewelled Treasures

Items of fine jewellery fashioned from precious metals and gemstones have an intrinsic material worth; they were often expensive to buy and are, at one level, a form of portable wealth. However, many personal jewels were also received as intimate tokens, or bestowed as romantic or affectionate gifts – precisely the kinds of valuable, meaningful possessions intended to be preserved.

Rings are common survivals in family collections, for example, women's engagement, marriage or eternity bands, or men's signet rings. These are often worn by several generations, sometimes being professionally refashioned to suit contemporary taste; in particular, during the 1950s to 1970s many older rings and brooches were re-set into modern forms. Other popular jewellery heirlooms include twentieth-century wristwatches or traditional pocket-watches, brooches and lockets on chains. Unless ancestors were affluent far back in time, most inherited jewellery pieces are mass-produced, machine-made items of Victorian or later date. Look out for these in old family photographs; they may well have been 21st-birthday, engagement or marriage presents. Hinged lockets often contain pictures of a loved one, or paired images – tiny photographs or painted miniatures dateable from their subjects' appearance. A lock of hair was sometimes contained in lockets too, not only that of deceased relatives, as is often assumed, but also the living – an affectionate souvenir.

Painted and Printed Records

Old photographs of relatives and ancestors are wonderful heirlooms and, as discussed in Chapter 2, in portraying earlier generations in their 'Sunday best' often link closely to fashion. Some family collections also contain framed or cased watercolour miniatures or larger oil paintings on canvas – original artworks created for more prosperous forebears. Privileged ancestors were usually literate at an early date: some wrote about their clothes and recorded portrait sittings, like Simon Martin's predecessor whose journal for 29 July 1845 states: 'I took my first sitting. I wore my ruby velvet.' (See coloured image No.4).

Family archives can include many kinds of surviving dress-related documents in printed or hand-written form, from descriptions in private letters, diaries, journals and memoirs, through household account books itemising clothing purchases, to orders, invoices, bills and receipts for goods or services rendered. Dress-related heirlooms are the ultimate family records – physical evidence of the prominent role played by fashion in our ancestors' lives.

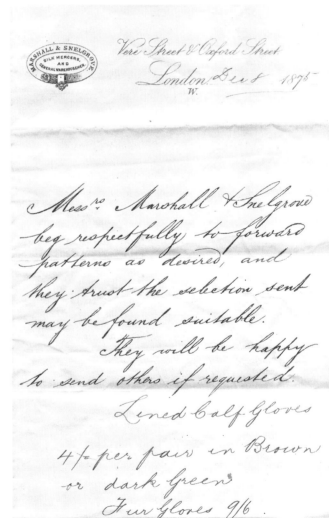

Family heirloom: Letter from Marshall & Snelgrove concerning gloves, December 1875.

Bibliography

Dress & Fashion History

Byrde, Penelope *The Male Image: Men's Fashion in England 1300–1970*, B.T. Batsford Ltd, 1979

Byrde, Penelope *A Visual History of Costume: The Twentieth Century*, B.T. Batsford Ltd, 1986

Byrde, Penelope *Nineteenth Century Fashion*, B.T. Batsford Ltd, 1992

Byrde, Penelope *Jane Austen Fashion: Fashion and Needlework in the Works of Jane Austen*, Moonrise Press, 2008

Cunnington, Phillis & Mansfield, Alan *English Costume for Sports and Outdoor Recreation*, Adam & Charles Black, 1969

Ehrmann, Edwina *The Wedding Dress: 300 Years of Bridal Fashions*, V&A Publishing, 2014

Emery, Joy Spanabel *A History of the Paper Pattern Industry: The Home Dressmaking Fashion Revolution*, Bloomsbury, 2014

Ewing, Elizabeth *History of Children's Costume*, B.T. Batsford Ltd, 1977

Foster, Vanda *A Visual History of Costume: The Nineteenth Century*, B.T. Batsford Ltd, 1984

Gernsheim, Alison *Victorian and Edwardian Fashion: A Photographic Survey*, Dover Publications, 1981

Horwood, Catherine *Keeping up Appearances: Fashion and Class between the Wars*, Sutton Publishing, 2005

Marly, Diana de *Working Dress: A History of Occupational Clothing*, B.T. Batsford Ltd, 1986

Milford-Cottam, Daniel *Edwardian Fashion*, Shire Publications, 2014

Richmond, Vivienne *Clothing the Poor in Nineteenth-Century England*, Cambridge University Press, 2013

Rose, Clare *Children's Clothes*, B.T. Batsford Ltd, 1989

Shrimpton, Jayne *British Working Dress: Occupational Clothing 1750–1950*, Shire Publications, 2012

Shrimpton, Jayne *Fashion in the 1920s*, Shire Publications, 2013

Shrimpton, Jayne *Fashion in the 1940s*, Shire Publications, 2014

Shrimpton, Jayne *Victorian Fashion*, Shire Publications, 2016

Taylor, Lou *Mourning Dress: A Costume and Social History*, Routledge Revivals, 2009

Tobin, Shelley et al *Marriage à la Mode: Three Centuries of Wedding Dress*, The National Trust, 2003

Toplis, Alison *The Clothing Trade in Provincial England, 1800–1850*, Pickering & Chatto, 2011

Walkley, Christina and Foster, Vanda *Crinolines and Crimping Irons – Victorian Clothes: How They Were Cleaned and Cared For*, Peter Owen Publishers, 1978

Wilson, Elizabeth & Taylor, Lou *Through the Looking Glass: A History of Dress from 1860 to the Present Day*, BBC Books, 1989

Wilson, Elizabeth *Adorned in Dreams: Fashion and Modernity*, I.B. Tauris & Co Ltd, Rev. ed. 2009

Worth, Rachel *Discover Dorset: Dress and Textiles*, The Dovecote Press, 2002

Worth, Rachel *Clothing and Landscape in Victorian England*, Bloomsbury, 2018

Family Photographs

Linkman, Audrey *The Victorians: Photographic Portraits*, Tauris Parke, 1993

Shrimpton, Jayne *Family Photographs and How to Date Them*, Countryside Books, 2008

Shrimpton, Jayne *How to Get the Most from Family Pictures*, Society of Genealogists, 2011

Shrimpton, Jayne *Tracing Your Ancestors through Family Photographs*, Pen & Sword, 2016

Occupations & Trades

Bythell, Duncan, *The Sweated Trades: Outwork in Nineteenth-Century Britain*, Harper Collins, 1978

Cox, Pamela & Hobley, Annabel *Shopgirls: The True Story of Life Behind the Counter*, Hutchinson, 2014

Emm, Adèle *My Ancestors Worked in Textile Mills*, Society of Genealogists, 2019

Emm, Adéle *Tracing Your Trade & Craftsmen Ancestors*, Pen & Sword, 2015

Freeman, Charles *Luton and the Hat Industry*, Luton Museum & Art Gallery, 1976

Malcolmson, Patricia *English Laundresses: 1850–1930*, University of Illinois Press, 1986

Palmer, Marilyn *Framework Knitting*, Shire Publications, 2002

Pennington, Shelley & Westover, Belinda *A Hidden Workforce: Homeworkers in England, 1850–1985*, MacMillan Education, 1989

Redwood, Mike *Gloves and Glove-Making*, Shire Publications, 2016

Teasdale, Vivien *Tracing Your Textile Ancestors*, Pen & Sword, 2009

Original sources

Bell, Lady Florence *At the Works: Study of a Manufacturing Town (1907)*, Leopold Classic Library, 2016

Mayhew, Henry *London Labour and the London Poor*, Wordsworth Classics, 2008

Reeves, Maud Pember *Round About a Pound a Week*, Persephone Books Ltd, 2008

Thompson, Flora *Lark Rise to Candleford: A Trilogy*, Oxford University Press, 1945

Index